PRAISE FOR
BOOKSMART

"Buy it; read it; live it. Then you'll want to give copies to those you really care about. I guarantee you won't regret it."
— **BOB VANOUREK**
Award-winning author and five-times corporate CEO

"If you buy only one book this year, get *BOOKSMART*. It simplifies the complicated, and it gives meaningful answers to our questions about success and happiness."
— **LOLLY DASKAL**
Founder and President, Lead From Within
"One of The Most Inspiring Women in the World!" *The Huffington Post*

"Awesome! *BOOKSMART* will provide you with powerful ideas and tools for creating a more meaningful and rewarding life."
— **JOHN SPENCE**
"Among Top 500 Leadership Development Experts in the World." HR.com

"Witty, incisive, and profound! I highly recommend this book to anyone who realizes that mastering success begins with mastering oneself."
— **AUGUST TURAK**
Author, *Business Secrets of the Trappist Monks*

"As a professional book reviewer for various eminent international journals, I read thousands of books. This is definitely one of the most inspiring! I strongly recommend it."
PROFESSOR M.S. RAO, PhD
Father of "Soft Leadership" and the author of 30 books

PRAISE FOR BOOKSMART

"Are you book-smart or street-smart? The best in business are both! In this terrific collection of leadership insights, Frank shares the secrets you need to serve — and lead — in your life and work."
— **JAMES STROCK**
Author, *Serve to Lead*

"No one should be without Frank's beautiful pearls of wisdom. They're like hugs that propel you toward your dreams."
— **SARAH HINER**
President and CEO, Bottom Line Inc. (Publisher of *Bottom Line Personal*)

"Any one of the subjects Frank writes about offers a valuable life lesson. But when you combine them all in one book, they pack a powerful punch that makes BOOKSMART priceless."
— **CATHERINE LEPONE**
Executive Director, Youth Development Organization

"*BOOKSMART* is full of ideas that will help enrich your character — it provides the inspiration and motivation to be the best possible you."
— **AMY SMIT**
Associate Director, The Ray Center (Formerly Character Counts in Iowa)

"Frank Sonnenberg is one of the most respected thought leaders of our times. He has the gift of imparting profound life lessons in practical, inspiring stories that we all can relate to."
— **MELANIE GREENBERG, PhD**
Clinical Psychologist
Expert Blogger, *Psychology Today*

BOOKSMART

Hundreds of **real-world** lessons
for success and happiness

FRANK SONNENBERG

Printed in the United States of America.

ISBN-13: 978-1535233385
ISBN-10: 1535233389

Library of Congress Control Number: 2016911515
CreateSpace Independent Publishing Platform, North Charleston, SC

Cover and interior design by Carrie Ralston, Simple Girl Design LLC.

TO MY WIFE, AND BEST FRIEND, CARON

— I love you just the way you are.

and

TO CATHERINE, ERIC, KRISTINE, AND JOHN

— Live a life of purpose.
Care not only about where life has taken you,
but about how you got there as well.
Remember that happiness is as important as success.

CONTENTS

ACKNOWLEDGMENTS

*B*ookSmart was made possible by a wonderful and talented group of people who embody the values that are depicted in this book.

Caron Sonnenberg is my wife and my best friend. Caron is the first person to read and comment on my work. Her thoughts are invaluable. They're astute, honest, and sensible. Thank you so much for your encouragement, support, and patience while I wrote this book. The wedding song that we danced to years ago still applies today. Caron, "I love you just the way you are."

Carrie Ralston, Simple Girl Design LLC, is an incredible person and a gifted art director. She designed the cover and the interior of this book. Furthermore, she designed my blog and continues to support it each day. I've worked with many, many art directors in the course of my career. Carrie is among the very best. She is talented beyond words and true to her own personal values. Carrie, I consider it a privilege and an honor to work with you each day. You're one in a million.

Kathy Dix is a knowledgeable, caring, and hardworking professional. I have worked with Kathy for over 10 years. She reviews and comments on every manuscript that I write before it sees daylight. I've come to rely heavily on Kathy's thoughtful and sage advice and continue to be in awe of her incredible talent. Kathy, thank you so much for being so good at your craft. I couldn't have completed this book without you.

Eric Wagner, Fifth Cup LLC, is a competent, experienced, and hardworking IT professional. He works his magic so that our blog runs smoothly each day. Eric embodies all the excellent personal qualities and values that I discuss in this book. Eric, when you're on the job, I sleep well at night. You make a tough job look easy.

Last, but not least, several of the lessons in this book were collaborations with friends. They include the following: *Living in the Fast Lane*, Alan D. Hembrough; *Winging It Through Life*, David A. Tierno; *Live with Honor and Integrity* and *The Secret to True Happiness*, Edward Berryman.

• • •

I consider myself to be the luckiest man in the world. I'm blessed with an awesome family, surrounded by caring friends, living a fairy-tale marriage, and have had a wonderful career. I'd like to recognize a few people who have helped to shape my character and have contributed so much to making my life rewarding and meaningful.

When I think about outstanding mentors, my good friend Mark Sandberg, PhD, comes to mind. If I said that Mark is an extraordinary mentor, I'd be understating his contribution. Mark is a consummate teacher, so it was only natural that he became a college professor — capping off his career as a business school Dean. While there are many professors in the world, there's only one Mark. He intuitively knew the true potential of his students and made it his mission to bring out the best in them. This may not seem unusual for a teacher, except that Mark mentored hundreds of students inside and outside the classroom. He never did it for money, to feather his ego, or to receive anything in return. Mark did it for no other reason than the simple fact that he gains more satisfaction from others' success than from his own. I, like so many others, am forever grateful for his selflessness. To this day, he doesn't realize the impact that he had on the lives of so many. I consider myself very fortunate that Mark is a part of my life.

When I think about exceptional leadership, my mentor, Dave Tierno, former Senior Partner, Management Consulting Group, Ernst & Young (EY), comes to mind. I worked for Dave for over a decade and learned so much from him. Dave represents everything that you'd ever hope for in a leader. Dave is principled, realistic, determined, decisive, fair and open-minded, humble...the list can go on. Dave never had to pull rank or resort to command and control to get results. He led Ernst & Young's Management Consulting Group to new heights because he was knowledgeable, admired, trusted, and respected. I haven't worked for Dave in over 25 years and I would still move heaven and earth for him.

When I think about the importance of honor and integrity, my good friend Larry Frankel comes to mind. I've known Larry for over 30 years. He achieved success the old-fashioned way: he earned it. Larry is brilliant, hardworking, trustworthy, and selfless. He worked his way up from humble beginnings to become one of the leading financial advisors in the country. Larry is successful beyond words, but you'd never know it. That's because he never forgot his roots. Larry is living proof that there's a direct correlation between integrity and success. I'm honored to call him and his wife, Debbie, my friends.

When I think about living the American Dream, my good friend Denis Salamone comes to mind. Denis was raised in a middle-class family where family, character, education, and hard work were emphasized and valued. These principles served him well as he worked his way up the corporate ladder to become Partner and serve on the Board of Partners of Pricewaterhouse-Coopers. Denis later became Chairman and CEO of one of the nation's largest banks and now serves on the Board of Directors of M&T Bank. Denis and his wife, Jody, continue to reinforce the same values with their family that they received from their parents. They remember their roots, give generously to their community, and keep the important things in life in perspective. Thank you both for being such good friends.

When I think about role models, my good friend Ed Berryman comes to mind. Ed doesn't talk about personal values; he and his wife, Joanne, live them. They're honorable people, loving parents, caring friends, and strong community-minded individuals. Most important, it's very evident that Ed and Joanne passed their values on to their children. When you meet their family it's very clear that the apple doesn't fall far from the tree.

My mother and father were wonderful role models who instilled the strong values in me that are so much a part of this book. My brothers and I grew up in a household where honesty and integrity presided over all else, where people's wealth was measured by their character rather than their material possessions, and where people got more joy out of giving than from asking for more. My parents instilled in us the confidence that we could be anyone or do anything as long as we had the courage and the will to achieve our dreams.

There's nothing more gratifying in life than watching your kids grow up to be principled human beings living up to their potential. We're so proud of the young ladies that our daughters, Catherine and Kristine, have become. We're also thrilled that their husbands, Eric and John, have joined our family. Finding your soul mate in life is so important. Caron and I couldn't have chosen better guys for our daughters if we tried. Our dream is that you live a life filled with happiness and offer the same to your kids one day. To that end, I hope that this book offers some guidance on how to achieve success and happiness. We love you all very much.

Caron is the love of my life. We've been married for 36 years, and I love her as much today as when I first laid eyes on her. We raised a family, built a business together, and literally spend all our free time together. And the funny thing is that I never get tired of being with her. Caron, you wear many hats. You're my wife, confidante, co-parent, and best friend. As I said earlier, I feel like I'm the luckiest person in the world. That's because I met you. I guess they call that love.

Thank you all.

Follow your conscience.
Sleep well.

MAKE EVERY MOMENT MATTER

EVERYONE WAS PUT ON THIS EARTH FOR A REASON. **WHAT'S YOURS?**

FIND YOUR PURPOSE AND PURSUE YOUR PASSION WITH GUSTO.

BELIEVE IN THE IMPOSSIBLE BECAUSE EVERYTHING SEEMS IMPOSSIBLE UNTIL YOU PROVE THAT IT CAN BE DONE.

REACH FOR THE STARS AND BE PROUD OF YOUR ACHIEVEMENTS, BUT ALSO TAKE PRIDE IN THE WAY THAT YOU ACHIEVE THEM.

MAKE GOOD CHOICES BECAUSE YOUR LIFE WILL GROW TO BE THE SUM OF THOSE DECISIONS.

DO WHAT'S RIGHT, NOT OUT OF FEAR OF GETTING CAUGHT, BUT BECAUSE INTEGRITY MATTERS. YOU HAVE TO LIVE WITH YOURSELF FOR THE REST OF YOUR LIFE.

MAKE A DIFFERENCE IN PEOPLE'S LIVES, NOT BECAUSE YOU EXPECT SOMETHING IN RETURN, BUT BECAUSE WITNESSING THEIR HAPPINESS IS, BY ITSELF, A WORTHY REWARD.

FIND YOUR HAPPINESS, NOT BY MEANS OF SEEKING MORE, BUT BY APPRECIATING WHAT YOU ALREADY HAVE.

COLLECT MEMORIES BECAUSE THINGS MAY OFFER A MOMENT'S PLEASURE, BUT YOU'LL CHERISH YOUR MEMORIES FOREVER AND EVER.

MAKE EVERY MOMENT MATTER.

FRANK SONNENBERG

LIFE LESSONS

It's your life to live.
Own it!

You have to live with
yourself for the rest
of your life.

IT'S YOUR LIFE TO LIVE. OWN IT!

Everyone is born with the potential for greatness. What happens next is up to you. You get to choose which path you take, how high to set the bar for yourself, and how hard you're willing to work to clear it. You get to decide how to spend your time, who to spend it with, and what you're willing to forgo when time runs short. Every choice that you make and every action that you take has consequences, but who better to decide what's best for you — than you. It's your life to live. Own it!

Securing the ultimate prize takes strength and courage. You're going to face challenges that seem insurmountable and suffer setbacks along the way, but faith, hard work, and determination will see you through. Don't listen to naysayers or allow others to lead you astray; follow your heart and let your dreams lead the way. You owe it to yourself to be the best you can be. You'll travel this road only once. Believe in yourself and make yourself proud. There are no dress rehearsals in life.

WORDS TO LIVE BY

Here are 14 guideposts for your journey through life:

Be your own person. Get real; be yourself. Consider the advice of others, but trust yourself in the end.

Make yourself proud. Do your best; nothing less. Set standards of excellence that make the most important person — you — proud.

Keep good company. Surround yourself with positive people who genuinely care about your well-being and bring out the best in you.

Find your passion. Pursue your dreams with fervor, and put your heart into everything you do. Everyone was put on this earth for a purpose… what's yours?

Make a difference. Be a positive force in people's lives. It doesn't require a gift from your wallet but rather, a caring heart.

Prioritize your activities. Focus on the things that matter most. Everything on your plate isn't of equal importance.

Invest your time. Think of time as your most valuable currency, and invest it wisely.

Be accountable. Accept responsibility for your behavior. When things go well, accept your well-deserved rewards. When they don't, admit fault, learn from your mistakes, and move on.

Face reality. Be the change that you want to be. If you look in the mirror and don't like what you see, don't blame the mirror.

Invest in yourself. Don't stop educating yourself. Learn something new every day. You'll be able to leverage that investment for the rest of your life.

Be grateful. Appreciate what you have, while you have it, or you'll learn what it meant to you after you've lost it.

Make lots of memories. Take time to smell the roses. *Possessions* age and lose value over time; *memories* last forever.

Remain true to your values. Compromise on your position, but not your principles. Listen to your conscience. That's why you have one.

Guard your reputation. Protect your reputation like it's the most valuable asset you own. Because it is!

LIVE THE DREAM

Success and happiness don't just happen by chance; you have to go out and earn them for yourself. No one says they're simple or easy to attain; it takes courage, hard work, and dedication. The key is to set high standards, remain true to your values, listen to your conscience, and never stop trying. At the end of the day, it's your life to live. Own it! You have to live with yourself for the rest of your life. **:)**

"

People who live
a life of purpose have
core beliefs and values
that influence their
decisions, shape their
day-to-day actions,
and determine their
short- and long-term
priorities.

"

7 WAYS TO LIVE LIFE WITH A PURPOSE

Some people measure success by the wealth they've accumulated, the power they've attained, or the status they've achieved. Yet, even though they've reached success beyond their wildest dreams, they still have an empty feeling — something is missing from their life. In order to fill that void and be completely fulfilled in life, their soul may be searching for something more.

Here are a few scenarios that describe this emptiness:

Lonely at the top. I was obsessed with making it to the top. When I arrived, however, I learned that it wasn't all it was cracked up to be. I now realize that my continual pursuit of advancement seriously compromised my ability to spend quality time with my family and build meaningful relationships with friends.

Enough is never enough. One of the ways I kept score in life was to compare my toys to my neighbors' toys. It felt good for a while, but each "high" just didn't last. I now know better. I realize that if I'm not careful, the game of life can become an obsession — there will always be people with more and less than I have.

Sold my soul. I would have given anything to be a success. I lied, cheated, and sold my soul to the devil. I understand now that although I've obtained fame and fortune, people don't like or respect me. Knowing what I've done, I find it hard to live with myself, and others seem to agree.

All work and no play. I was always the first person in the office and the last one to leave. While my business life has been a roaring success, my personal life has been a disaster. I realize there's got to be more to life. Balance matters, and I must be the one to make it happen.

Pleased everyone except myself. I never made a move without first seeking the approval of my friends and family. They're happy, but I'm miserable. I now appreciate that my opinion matters, too, and counting on others to make up my mind for me is just a cop-out.

Lived in the future rather than the present. I spent much of my life thinking about what I was going to do tomorrow. Now that I'm older, I've come face-to-face with the reality that my days won't go on forever; I wish I had learned to savor every special moment as it happened.

If any of these scenarios sound familiar to you, it may be time for a course correction.

LIVING LIFE WITH A PURPOSE

Live by your beliefs and values. People who live a life of purpose have core beliefs and values that influence their decisions, shape their day-to-day actions, and determine their short- and long-term priorities. They place significant value on being a person of high integrity and in earning the trust and respect of others. The result is that they live with a clear conscience and spend more time listening to their inner voice than being influenced by others.

Set priorities. People who live a life of purpose identify those activities that matter most to them and spend the majority of their time and effort in those areas. Otherwise, it's too easy to drift away in the currents of life. As Annie Dillard, the author, once said, "How we spend our days is, of course, how we spend our lives."

Follow your passion. People who live a life of purpose wake up each morning eager to face the new day. They pursue their dreams with fervor, put their heart into everything they do, and feel that they're personally making a difference. As James Dean, the actor, once said, "Dream as if you'll live forever. Live as if you'll die today."

Achieve balance. People who live a life of purpose put their heart into their career and into building relationships with friends and family. They also reserve adequate time to satisfy their personal needs. Achieving balance means living up to one's potential in all facets of life.

Feel content. People who live a life of purpose have an inner peace. They're satisfied with what they have and who they are. To them, the grass is greener on their own side of the fence. As the saying goes, "The real measure of your wealth is how much you'd be worth if you lost all your money."

Make a difference. People who live a life of purpose make a meaningful difference in someone else's life. They do things for others without expectation of personal gain, and they gain as much satisfaction from witnessing the success of others as from witnessing their own. As the old proverb says, "A candle loses nothing by lighting another candle."

Live in the moment. People who live a life of purpose cherish every moment and seek to live life without regret. They take joy in the experiences that life gives and don't worry about keeping score. Dr. Seuss may have said it best, "Don't cry because it's over. Smile because it happened." **:)**

"

Measuring progress is often like watching grass grow. While it's difficult to detect movement on a daily basis, it's simple to see growth over time.

"

MAKE BIG STRIDES WITH SMALL STEPS

Most of us like to see progress right away. So, when we take baby steps and can't detect advancement, we abandon our efforts, thinking that we've failed. The truth is, measuring progress is often like watching grass grow. While it's difficult to detect movement on a daily basis, it's simple to see growth over time. Here are nine guidelines to keep the grass green on your side of the fence:

Multiply your success — or failure. The law of compounding can turn a small sum into a fortune. Albert Einstein said, "Compound interest is the eighth wonder of the world. He who understands it, earns it...he who doesn't...pays it." The same is true of your small steps.

Get better every day. School shouldn't be the end of the learning process. Personal excellence requires a strong desire and disciplined learning on a continual basis. One day, someone may ask how you became such an expert in an area. You'll probably say that you acquired the knowledge and experience little by little over the years.

Nag, Nag, Nag. You never know when you're teaching your kids a life lesson. It could be a comment during a ball game or the way that you personally reacted to a situation. The best way to instill proper values is to promote them, on a *continual* basis, and reinforce your words with your actions.

Create good habits. One way to correct a bad habit is to take small steps rather than make a bold move. Small steps are realistic and require less willpower. Short-term wins will motivate you to continue on your journey.

Get a lifestyle. Some people want good health as long as it doesn't require them to abandon bad habits. Instead, they resort to quick-fix remedies that require minimal personal sacrifice. The truth is, you can't live an *unhealthy* lifestyle and expect a *healthy* outcome.

Address larger-than-life problems. Do you get overwhelmed by large challenges? If that sounds familiar, break big problems into small, manageable pieces. Each piece may seem small, but the combination of these pieces will yield big results.

Make downtime uptime. How often do you find yourself waiting fifteen minutes for others? Most people believe nothing meaningful can be accomplished during that time. The fact is, you can be very productive by completing small, related tasks that, when combined, complete a large undertaking.

Waste not, want not. Some people think that cutting small items in a budget isn't worthy of their effort. The truth is, many small cuts can make a huge difference.

Win back trust. Some people think trust can be repaired overnight. The fact is, trying to swing for the fence may only compound the problem. The best way to repair an indiscretion is to be deliberate, consistent, and most of all, worthy.

SMALL STEPS MAKE A BIG DIFFERENCE

Small steps today yield great rewards tomorrow. These are seven principles to guide you through the process.

Make the long-term investment. Every major undertaking requires desire, sacrifice, patience, and determination. Remember, it takes many years to become an overnight success.

Win in the short and long term. It's important to set ambitious, yet realistic, short-term goals as you pursue your long-term interests. Remember, small wins provide momentum while long-term goals enable you to win big.

Establish a clear goal. Before beginning any task, ask yourself, "Is this activity instrumental to achieving my goal?" That's because random activities can be wasteful or even work at cross-purposes with each other. Remember, when tasks work in concert, progress is compounded.

Walk before you run. If you don't make the investment, don't expect the rewards. People will place their trust in you *only after* testing your motives; people rise to the top of an organization *only after* proving themselves at the bottom.

Just say "no." The goal shouldn't always be adding to, but should sometimes also be subtracting from daily tasks. While any single request may seem reasonable, added together these requests will divert your attention from your priorities.

Measure activity rather than progress. Sometimes it's difficult, if not impossible, to detect progress. So have faith that positive activity leads to positive results.

Think small. Fight the urge to overthink everything. Get started. Don't try to get it perfect. It's more important to get a few words down on paper and clean up the draft afterward.

SUCCESS IS ONE SMALL STEP AWAY

Did you ever hear a doctor say an illness is the result of years of personal neglect? What he or she is saying is that the sum of our choices and actions *yesterday* came home to roost *today*. It only stands to reason that the same prescription applies to other areas of our life. Every small thing that we do today is an investment in our future. The investment may not pay off for years. But if you don't begin today, you may live to regret it tomorrow.

As Robert Louis Stevenson said, "Don't judge each day by the harvest you reap, but by the seeds that you plant." The fact is, success is a game of inches. When you do something well day in and day out, the cumulative impact is huge. So dream big, but think one small step at a time. **:)**

"

Checking items off a to-do list doesn't determine progress; focusing on your priorities is what counts.

"

IS YOUR TO-DO LIST OVERWHELMING YOU?

Did you ever feel that your to-do list was so out of control that it triggered a mental or physical response? Your hands got clammy, your heart started pounding, and your anxiety level reached a new height.

It's so easy for a to-do list to snowball out of control. In some cases, it takes no time at all to go from "I can do this," to outright panic. In fact, it can become so overwhelming that it makes you freeze in your tracks — preventing you from getting *anything* done. "How can it get this bad?" you ask. One word…procrastination.

HOW PROCRASTINATION DESTROYS PROGRESS

People procrastinate by putting things off rather than working on them. This causes things to build up to the point where they're no longer manageable. As Professor Mason Cooley said, "Procrastination makes easy things hard, hard things harder." Here are twelve reasons why folks procrastinate:

Lack of discipline. "I'll do this some other time."

Fear of failure. "I'm not sure I can do this. So I won't even try."

Wishful thinking. "If I don't think about it, maybe it'll go away."

Unreasonable expectations. "If I can't guarantee success, I won't even attempt it."

Feeling overwhelmed. "This project seems daunting. Let me give it some thought…tomorrow."

Fear of complexity. "I'm not sure where to begin."

Lack of motivation. "I'm not in the mood."

Fear of accountability. "I'm afraid to put my neck on the line."

Feeling bored. "I'd rather be doing something else."

Lack of urgency. "It really doesn't matter if I do it now. It's not due for days."

Fear of making a decision. "I need more information before I can start."

Wait till the last minute. "I love the adrenaline rush that I get when I'm up against a deadline."

HOW TO TACKLE YOUR TO-DO LIST

Here are eight strategies to help you get it done:

Start with priorities. Remember, everything on your to-do list is *not* a priority. Checking items off a to-do list doesn't determine progress; focusing on your priorities is what counts.

Don't give it a second thought. Sometimes the hardest thing to do is to get started. So fight the urge to overthink everything. Jump right in without delay.

Limit distractions. Don't let anything or anyone sidetrack you. Focus on your task at hand. Whatever is "calling" you will be there when you're finished.

Learn from mistakes. Be aware of how you procrastinate and learn from it. When people don't learn from mistakes, their actions often turn into bad habits.

Set a short-term goal. Make a commitment to yourself — even an artificial deadline. A goal forces us to get things done.

Break big activities down into small pieces. Don't get overwhelmed by the magnitude of a task. Big problems are best solved in small pieces.

Fire the perfectionist. You'll rarely have all the information you need to make a "perfect" decision. So don't demand perfection. The philosopher Voltaire warned against letting the perfect be the enemy of the good. That advice still holds true today.

Think about it. Be conscious of your thoughts. Try to replace counter-productive thoughts with positive ones that motivate you and keep you on task.

MAKE IT HAPPEN

Did you ever see airplanes lining up for their final approach to an airport? It looks like ballet in the sky. Although it's fun to watch, you can imagine the timing and split-second decisions that must be made to land the airplanes safely. Could you imagine what would happen if the air traffic controllers procrastinated?

Although our to-do list contains very few life-and-death decisions, each item should be tackled with the same speed, agility, and thoughtfulness. That means maintaining the right perspective, committing to the goal, focusing on the task, and getting it done. The truth is, air traffic controllers don't have time to get overwhelmed, make excuses, or put off decisions for another day. Air traffic controllers have a job to do. You do too! So take command of your to-do list and land your airplanes. **:)**

"

A positive mental attitude can improve your health, enhance your relationships, increase your chances of success, and add years to your life.

"

IT PAYS TO BE POSITIVE

Most people are bombarded by negativity each day. Sure, it's easy to cast blame by saying you're surrounded by negative people. The reality is that a lot of the negativity is self-inflicted…influenced by the company you keep and your perspective on life.

Let's take a closer look at the negativity that we face every day…

Arguments. Many arguments are the result of poor communication or the clash of opposing values and principles. People also argue to force their viewpoint on others or to just let off steam.

Worry. Many people worry about losing control. They desire certainty in an uncertain world.

Fear. Some folks fear the unknown. Whether their fear is real or imagined, perception is reality.

Blame. When something goes wrong, people often look to cast blame on others. The result is that people usually watch out for #1 — themselves — often at the expense of those others.

Complaints. Many people don't complain because they're unhappy. Compulsive complainers grumble out of boredom or a desire to turn an awkward moment of silence into a conversation starter. People also complain because it makes them feel better to vent.

Criticism. There's a difference between constructive feedback and biting criticism. While constructive feedback is offered with good intent, constant and biting criticism can lead to stress, anxiety, and reduced self-esteem.

Mistrust. How much time is wasted and ill will created as a result of mistrust? People spend endless hours second-guessing intent, peering over their shoulders, and creating elaborate approval processes to check and recheck.

Jealousy. When is enough, enough? We live in a society where many people aren't satisfied with their own accomplishments. The grass always seems greener on the other side of the fence.

Gossip (our national pastime). People gossip to fit into a group, fill a void in conversation, prove that they're in the know, take revenge on a person, put someone in their place, or merely to gain attention.

IT PAYS TO BE POSITIVE

A positive mental attitude can improve your health, enhance your relationships, increase your chances of success, and add years to your life.

Here are several ways to adopt a positive attitude:

Surround yourself with positive people. Spend time with people who are positive and supportive. Remember, if you get too close to a drowning victim, he may take you down with him.

Be positive yourself. If you don't want to be surrounded by negative people, what makes you think others do? Learn to master your own thoughts. For example:

- When you visualize a goal, it makes you more likely to take the actions necessary to reach it. Visualize yourself winning the race, getting the promotion, accepting the award, or landing the new account.

- Control your negative thinking. This can be accomplished in the following ways:

    ○ See the glass as half full.

    ○ Anticipate the best outcome.

- Don't view everything in extremes — as either fantastic or a catastrophe. This will help you reduce your highs and lows.

- Mistakes happen. Negative people blame themselves for every bad occurrence, whether it was their fault or not. Don't let this be you.

Consciously resist negative thinking. Be cognizant of and mentally avoid negative thinking. This will help you modify your behavior.

Be nice to yourself. If you criticize yourself long enough, you'll start to believe it. This negativity can drag you down. It may be time to fire the critic and hire the advocate.

Set realistic, achievable goals. Build confidence by setting realistic goals and by hitting a lot of singles rather than swinging for the fences.

Keep it in perspective. Life is all about prioritizing the things that matter most in your life and focusing your efforts in these areas. Don't let trivial things get you down. Learn to address or ignore small issues and move on. It's time to sweat the big stuff.

Turn challenges into opportunities. Instead of letting challenges overwhelm you, turn them into opportunities. (Rather than hitting the wall, climb over it or go around.)

Count your blessings. Be grateful for the special things in your life rather than taking them for granted. Some people do this by giving thanks around the dinner table, keeping a written journal, or posting one special item each day on social media. Remember, some of the greatest possessions in life are free. Take every opportunity to make a wonderful new memory.

If you want to achieve happiness, better health, stronger relationships, and continued success, you may not have to look any further than the mirror. As the saying goes, "The happiest people don't necessarily have the best of everything; they just make the best of everything they have." Do you see the glass as half full or half empty? True happiness may depend on how you view the world and whom you look to for inspiration. It pays to be positive. **:)**

"

If you stop focusing
on all the reasons
why you can't do it,
you just may surprise
yourself to see what
you can do.

"

GET IT DONE!

What happens when someone asks us to do something really tough? First, we try to get out of it. Right? Next, we complain that they're asking the impossible. Then we whine to our friends, "I'm having such a bad day" or "The world is unfair." After we've exhausted every way to get out of the work…we take a break. (It's exhausting.) When we return, we brainstorm excuses to cover our behind if things go south. And when all else fails, and it usually does, we get down to work while grumbling to ourselves.

Contrast this mindset to a champion's approach…

I can hear the coach saying, "If they're bigger, be faster" "If they're better, play up." "If you're hurt, walk it off and then get back in the game." No whining, no excuses, and certainly no second-guessing. The players are positive, they're optimistic, and they're entirely focused on winning. These are the trademarks of winners. They'll do everything in their power, that's legitimate, to win. They know they have to "get it done."

Think about a soldier on a dangerous mission, a doctor saving a life, or a fire-fighter trying to pull a child from a burning building. They don't think, "I can't"; they don't complain "Why me"; and there's certainly no time for excuses. They put their head down and get it done.

How do you handle tough requests? Do you waste important energy complaining? Do you squander precious time making excuses? Does your defeatist attitude drag you down and kill the morale of your colleagues? Or do you think about all the things once considered impossible that are common-place today? Success begins with a can-do attitude.

Think about what you can accomplish if you set your mind to it. Next time you're faced with the "impossible," don't defeat yourself before you start. It takes a positive attitude to get things done. Rather than thinking "The deadline is impossible," "We don't have the resources," or "This has never been done before," put all your energy into making it happen. The truth is, if you stop focusing on all the reasons why you can't do it, you just may surprise yourself to see what you can do. Get it done! **:)**

Next time you're faced with the 'impossible,' don't defeat yourself before you start.

Given the option, would you rather choose the right path, even though it's difficult, or the easy route, knowing that you'll be compromising your standards?

THE EASY WAY MAY BE THE HARD WAY

How many times do we choose the easy route rather than the wise one? How many times do we close our eyes to wrongdoings even though we should speak our mind? How many times do we follow the crowd even though our conscience tells us to do otherwise? Are we simply taking the easy way out?

We're faced with decisions each day. Given the option, would you rather choose the *right* path, even though it's difficult, or the *easy* route, knowing that you'll be compromising your standards? The West Point cadet prayer* sums up their position well: "Make us to choose the harder right instead of the easier wrong."

EASY STREET IS FILLED WITH POTHOLES

Here are eleven examples of how we're tempted to choose convenience over principles:

It may be easier to:

- Sugarcoat bad news rather than tell it like it is.

- Sweep a problem under the rug rather than address the issue head-on.

- Create low expectations rather than set "stretch" goals.

- Look the other way rather than reprimand a star performer for unethical behavior.

- Point a finger rather than admit a mistake and learn a valuable lesson.

- Throw money at a problem rather than make good use of what we have.

- Follow the crowd rather than remain true to our beliefs and values.

- Promote a quick-fix solution rather than address a problem's root cause.

- Distribute resources equally rather than set priorities and make tough choices.

- Maintain silence rather than speak up for injustice.

- Encourage dependency rather than provide people with good opportunities as well as the tools to succeed.

EASIER SAID THAN DONE

Although our conscience often knows the right course to take, that doesn't mean we always choose the correct path. Here are six guiding principles for your journey through life:

That's easy for you to say. It's not enough to know the difference between right and wrong. The important thing is to convert those principles into words and actions. As the popular saying goes, "An ounce of action is worth a ton of theory."

Bad actions are habit-forming. Compromising your principles, even one time, can be a terrible mistake. As the saying goes, "Watch your thoughts, for they become words. Watch your words, for they become actions. Watch your actions, for they become habits. Watch your habits, for they become your character. And watch your character, for it becomes your destiny!"

Your future is determined today. The choices that you make today will impact your future. Live for today, but maintain a healthy balance between short-term success and building a better future.

Closing your eyes to problems won't make them disappear. It's important to run toward a problem rather than away from it. The truth is, small problems become big ones when left unattended.

Honor may come at a cost. People with strong moral character are selfless. While decisions are often beneficial long term, they can come with a short-term cost. For example, when you reprimand and sideline a star performer for unethical behavior, you're demonstrating the importance of integrity, but you may have to find another way to make up for that player's performance in the short term.

Actions have consequences. When you live with honor, you enable people to anticipate your behavior. This builds trust, confidence, and respect. More importantly, you can proudly face yourself in the mirror at the end of the day.

CHOOSE THE HARD RIGHT RATHER THAN THE EASY WRONG

It's one thing to know the difference between right and wrong and quite another to live your life that way. People with strong moral character set high standards, are true to their beliefs, and know that real success must be achieved the right way.

People with moral character believe that living with honor trumps anything that can possibly be gained by selling their soul. To them, success isn't about the fancy titles, luxurious toys, or celebrity status; living with honor offers a truly priceless reward — inner peace. The alternative, winning *without* honor, is worse than a resounding defeat.

People with strong moral character can't be influenced by opinion, enticed by temptation or intimidated by pressure. Furthermore, they don't need others to police their actions or second-guess their intent. People with strong moral character must answer to the toughest of all critics — their conscience. They are not driven by the desire to win at all costs but by the appeal of being true to oneself. They care not only about where life has taken them, but about how they got there. So the way I see it, the choice is easy. Will you choose the hard right rather than the easy wrong? Listen to your conscience. You have to live with yourself for the rest of your life. **:)**

*Source: http://www.usma.edu/chaplain/sitepages/cadet%20prayer.aspx

There's more to life than increasing its speed.

LIVING IN THE FAST LANE

In today's wonderful world of time-saving technologies, you'd think we'd be beneficiaries of an improved quality of life. More time for friends and family, more time to pursue personal interests, and more time to follow our dreams.

Wrong!

Despite these continuing advances, time saved has become time filled. Bombarded with added responsibilities, working families are faced with greater demands and obligations, increased stress levels, and tough choices to make between personal and professional commitments. In many cases, instead of living life to the fullest, we're living life on the edge — cramming as much as we can into a day, scrambling to get ahead, and running rampant on what sometimes seems to be a never-ending pursuit of the almighty buck.

This is life now that hyper-speed Internet communication has connected us to the demands of a hyper-speed world. One where tomorrow is not good enough for answers needed today. One where the pace of life that we once knew has changed forevermore, slamming us into high gear — full rev…with no time for idling. And often, no time for breathing.

Too often, our "must-do" lists do not include doing something for ourselves. Like hamsters, we live on a non-stop treadmill running pointlessly to nowhere, as moments pass us by. The scene of the "Norman Rockwell family" gathered together around the table has, in many instances, been replaced with that of working parents struggling to make ends meet. And children are being raised by others while we embrace a frantic daily work ritual. In short, we are becoming "absentee parents," losing opportunities to spend quality time with our children.

This is life.

Or, perhaps better stated…this is life?

Sadly, we are losing the priceless things that we once treasured. An extra hour or two to putter around the house, the joy of watching a child's first steps, or taking time to make our favorite chocolate chip cookies from scratch using grandma's recipe. And — home-cooked meals? Who has the time?

Today, those home-cooked meals we once enjoyed have been replaced by take-out dinners or a quick stop at the drive-through window. Family meals around the table have been reduced to grabbing a bite with anyone who happens to be home at the time, rather than "being a family" at least once during the day. Family conversations are fast disappearing, and what once was quality family time has now evolved to a drone-like fixation on a mega-sized TV screen, fighting for possession of the remote.

Even those special occasions we once anticipated and celebrated have been reduced in significance. For example, many holidays have become over-commercialized, and we find ourselves looking at them as "days off," rather than pausing to reflect on their true meaning and sharing them as a family, as a community, and as a united nation. And the care and time once spent thinking about buying, or making, just the right gift has, in many cases, been replaced with gift certificates — that is, if we can remember the occasion in the first place. These pleasures are often lost in the blur of living life in the fast lane, gone because we fail to hit the pause button and put our lives back into perspective. In many cases, we're becoming worker ants with tunnel vision.

The sobering fact is that there will come a point in time when we sit back, or more likely collapse in exhaustion, wondering what we've gained from this frenetic race called life. And in those moments of retrospection, will we really regret that missed promotion, the rejected proposal, or not being able to buy the bigger house? Or will we ponder our failed relationships — the feelings left unshared with someone we love, or the precious time lost with our children? Sadder yet, will we find ourselves living in a society where future generations accept these values as the norm?

ATTENTION, FELLOW HOMO SAPIENS!

This is your wake-up call before it's too late — the early warning signal to get a perspective on the things that matter.

Make time for yourself — if only just a few minutes — to reflect and regain some perspective — where you can redirect, realign, and realize a better, more rewarding life.

As authors, we find that we, too, are very much a part of this hyper-speed lifestyle that we're all living. We're no better than the next hardworking parent or individual trying to keep it all together. But, in our quieter moments, we do realize that there is a need to slow down…to put on the brakes and consider those values that are most important in life.

So take a moment to replenish your energies, re-establish your priorities, and re-introduce yourself to those things you once held close to your heart. There's more to life than increasing its speed. **:)**

Moral character
is the DNA of success
and happiness.

9 POWERFUL REASONS WHY YOUR MORAL CHARACTER MATTERS

It's not always easy to admit a mistake, persevere during tough times, or follow through on every promise made. It's not always comfortable to convey the hard truth or stand up for your beliefs. In the short term, it may not be beneficial to do right by your customers, to put people before profits, or to distance yourself from a questionable relationship. BUT, in the long run, doing the right thing is the clear path to both success and happiness.

Here are 9 powerful reasons why your moral character matters:

Achieve peace of mind. People with character sleep well at night. They take great pride in knowing that their intentions and actions are honorable. People with character also stay true to their beliefs, do right by others, and always take the high ground. (So refreshing.)

Strengthen trust. People with character enjoy meaningful relationships based on openness, honesty, and mutual respect. When you have good moral character, people know that your behavior is reliable, your heart is in the right place, and your word is good as gold.

Build a solid reputation. People with character command a rock-solid reputation. This helps them attract exciting opportunities "like a magnet."

Reduce anxiety. People with character carry less baggage. They're comfortable within their own skin, and they accept responsibility for their actions. They never have to play games, waste precious time keeping their stories straight, or invent excuses to cover their behind.

Increase leadership effectiveness. Leaders with character are highly effective. They have no need to pull rank or resort to command and control to get results. Instead, they're effective because they're knowledgeable, admired, trusted, and respected. This helps them secure buy-in automatically, without requiring egregious rules or strong oversight designed to *force* compliance.

Build confidence. People with character don't worry about embarrassment if their actions are publicly disclosed. This alleviates the need for damage control or the fear of potential disgrace as a result of indiscretions.

Become a positive role model. People with character set the standard for excellence. They live their life as an open book, teaching others important life lessons through their words and their deeds.

Live a purpose-driven life. People with character live a life they can be proud of. They're driven to make a difference and to do right by others rather than trying to impress others with extravagance. (Sounds like a wonderful legacy to me.)

Build a strong business. Doing the right thing is good business. Everything else being equal, talented people would rather work *for* — and customers would rather buy *from* — companies that do right by their people, customers, and communities. While following unprincipled business tactics may provide short-term results, it's NOT a long-term strategy.

Although you may not be able to quantify the benefits of being a good person, there's great truth in the saying, "good people finish first." Strong moral character is like a boomerang that causes good things to find their way back to you — but it takes effort. Jim Rohn, the business philosopher, said, "Character isn't something you were born with and can't change, like your fingerprints. It's something you weren't born with and must take responsibility for forming." So promise yourself to be true to yourself and do what's right, even when nobody is looking. — Moral character is the DNA of success and happiness. **:)**

"

Every time you give
your word, you're
putting your honor
on the line.

"

WHAT IS YOUR PROMISE WORTH?

M any people are pretty casual about making promises. As a result, promises are frequently made with no real intention of keeping them. "Let's do lunch," "I'll call you later," and "I'll be there in five minutes" are all examples of throwaway promises that are frequently made but seldom kept. The problem is that this casual attitude can have real consequences.

When you break a promise, no matter how small it may seem to you, alarm bells aren't going to go off, but it can damage a relationship or your reputation. Think about it — when someone breaks a promise to you, or gets caught in a lie, doesn't that make you feel violated or cheated? You can't help wondering whether you were wrong to ever trust that person in the first place.

PROMISE TO TELL THE WHOLE TRUTH

A promise is a promise. Some folks apply a rating scale, believing that breaking a *big* promise is inexcusable, while a *small* one is acceptable. That's simply false. While breaking a big promise, such as failing to repay borrowed money, can torpedo a relationship, reneging on small promises, such as being on time, casts doubt on future behavior.

Remember, trust is built through a series of experiences shared with others. When behavior is consistent, faith in the relationship develops. When promises are broken or people are misled, the bonds of trust are breached.

Broken promises imply that the offenders either didn't think before making the promises, or don't care that they've let you down. They're also implying that their needs are more important than yours. So be careful about the promises that you make and with whom you make them.

Never promise the moon. If you can't keep a promise, don't make it. For example, you may not be able to guarantee someone a five percent investment return, but you can show them your track record and promise that you'll work hard on their behalf. You can't guarantee that you'll arrive in two hours, but you can promise that you're going to leave at 10 a.m. You can't promise anyone sunny weather, but you can promise to hold the umbrella open for them if it rains.

Some broken promises are excusable. If you can't deliver something on time because of an uncontrollable event, such as a family illness, most people will understand that the lapse was unintentional. On the other hand, breaking a promise intentionally, such as failing to keep a secret, is different — there will be consequences.

When you distort the truth by exaggerating, spinning the truth, or withholding key facts, you also weaken your credibility for the future.

Half the truth is often a whole lie. Lying comes in many forms. Some people exaggerate or stretch the truth to make something look more attractive. Others "spin the truth" by presenting "selected" facts that support their position. Withholding key facts is also lying — it's clearly meant to deceive. When you tell a lie, everything that you say in the future may be treated as suspect. As Friedrich Nietzsche said, "I'm not upset that you lied to me, I'm upset that from now on I can't believe you."

You're judged by the company you keep. When people cover for the misdeeds of others, they're as guilty as those who committed the "crimes." If you're tempted to cover for someone else, first consider whether you're willing to put your reputation on the line for someone who's undeserving of your good name.

YOUR WORD IS YOUR BOND

There was a time when keeping your word held special significance. We took great pride in being of good character. Personal integrity was both expected and valued. That was a time when everyone knew each other's family, and you wouldn't do anything that would cast a shadow on your family's good name. It was a time when integrity was instilled in children at a very early age and was viewed as instrumental in achieving success. The truth is, our world may have changed, but the importance of integrity has not. While we may not know everyone in our own town, the world is still smaller than you think. Create some bad news and you'll learn this for yourself.

Every time you give your word, you're putting your honor on the line. You're implying that others can place their trust in you because you value integrity and would never let them down. It goes without saying that if you don't live up to your word, you may end up tarnishing your credibility, damaging your relationships, and defaming your reputation. Most importantly, you'll be letting yourself down.

But — when you operate with complete integrity, everything that you say will be taken at face value, your intentions will be assumed honorable, and your handshake will be as good as a contract. Most importantly, you can take great pride in the standards that you've set for yourself and sleep well at night knowing that your conscience is clear. As for others…just when they think they're fooling the world, they'll realize that they're only fooling themselves. After all, a promise is a promise. :)

Mistakes don't make you a failure, but beating yourself up makes you feel like one.

THE BIGGEST MISTAKE, EVER!

Mistakes have a negative image. So we hide them, play the blame game, or beat ourselves up when they occur. In fact, these actions compound our mistakes by creating stress and anxiety, damaging relationships, squandering time and money, and most importantly, often causing us to repeat the same mishap over and over again. The truth is, *mistakes aren't inherently bad — what counts is how we view and react to them.* How do you respond to mistakes? Do these actions sound familiar?

HOW DO YOU RESPOND TO MISTAKES?

Avoidance. Trying to avoid mistakes at any cost can be very costly. As Albert Einstein said, "A person who never made a mistake never tried anything new."

Repetition. When you run into a wall, don't dust yourself off and run into it again. Learn.

Inattention. Learn from other people's mistakes rather than reinventing the wheel — and making every mistake yourself.

Suppression. Sweeping mistakes under a rug never makes them really disappear.

Procrastination. Left unattended, small mistakes grow into big ones.

Judgment. Mistakes don't make you a failure, but beating yourself up makes you feel like one.

Dishonesty. It's one thing to make a mistake and quite another to commit one *intentionally* by being deceitful.

Denial. No one wins the blame game. Pointing fingers prohibits learning or progress from taking place. It's time to face the music.

Trapped. Dwelling in the past won't help you today.

VIEW MISTAKES AS AN OPPORTUNITY RATHER THAN A WEAKNESS

People fear mistakes because they're reprimanded and ridiculed for them. As a result, we become defensive when they occur. Imagine how we'd act if mistakes were a welcome way of life. As Ralph Nader said, "Your best teacher is your last mistake."

Encourage risk-taking. If mistakes were welcomed, you'd encourage risk-taking rather than defensive behavior. Mistakes would mean that you're setting "stretch goals" — leaving your comfort zone and attempting something new.

Welcome feedback. If mistakes were welcomed, you'd feel supported by constructive feedback rather than attacked by biting criticism. You'd feel exhilarated rather than stressed out.

Promote positive action. If mistakes were welcomed, you'd feel compelled to address the problem rather than afraid a mistake would be discovered. This would promote positive action rather than negativity.

Stimulate learning. If mistakes were welcomed, you'd feel comfortable sharing your mistakes rather than hiding from them. You'd know that sharing fosters learning. Why should other people have to learn from *their* mistakes when they can learn from *yours*?

Encourage teamwork. If mistakes were welcomed, you'd shift from a destructive to a positive environment. Finger-pointing and back-stabbing would give way to civility and mentoring.

Trusting partnerships. In business, if mistakes were transparent, communication with vendors would flourish and artificial walls would be torn down. Vendors would be treated more as allies than as adversaries.

MAKE NO MISTAKE ABOUT IT

When mistakes are made, our actions shift from doing the right thing to covering our behinds; to pointing fingers rather than accepting personal responsibility; hiding errors rather than fixing them; allowing wasteful projects to linger rather than shutting them down; and letting small problems become big ones because they're inadequately addressed. The result is that learning is brought to a complete standstill — making it more than likely the same mistake will be repeated. It shouldn't be that way.

The time has come to view every mistake as an opportunity rather than a weakness. This change in outlook will stimulate personal growth, strengthen relationships, and enhance efficiency and effectiveness. The truth is that there shouldn't be shame in making a mistake. The disgrace should be in failing to admit, correct, and learn from it. The bottom line is that the difference between mediocrity and exponential personal growth is how you view your mistakes. Make no mistake about it! **:)**

Learning is as much
an attitude as it is
an activity.

LIVE AND LEARN

Learning requires more than attending lectures and regurgitating what you've heard. It requires you to be both teacher and student, to learn from books and personal experiences, and to be able to apply lessons learned to real-world situations.

The great thing about self-directed, sometimes called informal, learning is that you own it. You determine what you want to learn, establish when the learning will take place, and have the opportunity to tailor it to your personal needs. There's no forced curriculum, there are no required exams, and there are absolutely no grades — except the ones you give yourself. Your only test is how much knowledge you're able to soak in and apply to your professional and personal life. Here are eight great ways to get started.

8 GREAT WAYS TO LEARN

Act like a kid. When we're young, we continually ask "why?" When we get older, however, we get defensive and feel inadequate if we don't have all the answers. It's time to learn like a kid again.

Broaden your world. Surrounding yourself with "yes" people is like talking to yourself. Listen to people with viewpoints other than your own. Try to see their side of the issue instead of living your life with blinders on.

Break out of the rut. Everyone likes routines. Learn by breaking them. Cover the same ground from different angles. Take a new route. Speak to new people. Get information from different sources.

Request feedback. Are you getting ready for a presentation or an interview? Don't be shy…request feedback from a colleague. Most people would be honored to help you. Remember, it's a lot better to learn in a non-threatening environment than when it's "game time."

Learn from mistakes. Do you have 20 years of experience or one year of experience repeated 20 times? If you're blind to your weaknesses, you may be repeating mistakes rather than correcting them. Remember, practice makes perfect — unless you're making the same mistakes over and over again.

Critique your actions. Football teams spend countless hours watching game footage to determine how to improve individual performance and build a winning team. Take the time to reflect on your experiences and learn from them. For example, ask yourself, "If I had the opportunity to perform that activity again, how would I do it differently?"

Increase your expectations. If you want to become a better tennis player, play with someone better than yourself. The same is true in other areas of your life. You're not going to improve if you don't accept challenges and learn from them. Step out of your comfort zone to "up" your game.

Remember that success is a journey, not a destination. Winning is not a black-and-white experience in which losers explore ways to improve and winners receive a bye. Even winners should identify ways to improve on their performance.

The world is at your fingertips. All you have to do is open your eyes and ears and begin taking it all in. The fact is, learning is as much an attitude as it is an activity. As the ancient proverb says, "When the student is ready, the teacher appears."

So promise yourself to begin today. Open your mind to new horizons — energize yourself by connecting with the world around you — and promise yourself that you'll strive for excellence. It'll change your perspective, it'll change your potential, and it'll change your life. Live and learn. **:)**

"

We're so busy
keeping busy that we
fail to see the error
of our ways.

"

DOING NOTHING IS TIME WELL SPENT

We live in a hyperactive world in which active lifestyles and overachievers are celebrated. In fact, we try to squeeze as much as we can into the day — with no time to spare. When we're not busy multitasking, we're racing from activity to activity. Right? So when was the last time you did nothing, simply because you thought doing nothing was time well spent?

The truth is, we're so busy keeping busy that it's easy to reach a point of diminishing returns — we lose more than we gain. You'd think we'd learn something from watching a hamster run around on a treadmill. What do we lose by constantly being on the run?

MAKE SOMETHING OUT OF NOTHING

Stop for a second. Take a deep breath. Are we busy to a fault?

Dream. Ever wonder why you get great ideas driving, in the shower, or running on the treadmill? Research shows that you're more likely to have an "aha!" moment when you're relaxed and allowing ideas to percolate in the back of your brain. So, to all the folks who eat lunch at their desk…it's time to take a break.

Reflect. Sometimes we're so busy doing stuff that we fail to consider whether it makes sense. Are we addressing what's important or what's next on our to-do list? Is there a better way to accomplish our goals? Stepping away from a situation often provides valuable perspective. Take the time to reflect.

Observe. Sometimes the best answer is right under our nose, but we're too busy to see it. If most answers seem obvious in retrospect, maybe we're not spending enough time searching for the obvious.

Bond. Clear your calendar. Spend a quiet evening with your spouse. Have dinner as a family rather than grabbing meals on the fly. Listen to your children today and be part of what they're doing tomorrow.

Relax. We work the whole year just to take a few days off. Then we spend vacations enjoying the simple life — relaxing on a beach, hiking through the woods, or watching a beautiful sunset. Why wait? Perhaps the only thing stopping you from relaxing is you. Instead of adding activities to your busy schedule, try eliminating some and then…relax.

Embrace life. When you spend your time counting every minute, you're bound to miss precious moments. Keep in mind that it's the moments, not the days, that you'll remember one day.

Show gratitude. Are you too busy to show the people in your life that you care? It doesn't take much effort and you'll certainly make their day.

Think. Some managers look at an employee staring out the window and think she's goofing off; others look at the same person and think, "Good, she's in deep thought." Think about that.

Learn. Kick off your shoes and learn something new. Explore new territory. Shift your focus. Open your mind. Leave familiar turf. Break out of the rut. See the big picture. Connect the dots. Change your outlook.

Recharge. Are you busy to a fault? Take some time to rejuvenate. Quiet your mind. Unplug. Meditate. Nap. Learn how to take a five-minute vacation.

Wander. Forget your aspirations for a moment. Take a walk to clear your head. Stroll without a purpose. Get lost within yourself. Who knows what you'll find.

NOTHING IS SOMETHING WORTH DOING

While some believe that keeping a frantic pace helps us accomplish more each day, the jury is still out. The only sure thing we may gain from our hectic lifestyle is stress and anxiety. Maybe it's time for this hamster to get off the treadmill. The truth is, we're so busy keeping busy that we fail to see the error of our ways. In fact, as Sydney J. Harris, the journalist, said, "The time to relax is when you don't have time for it."

Life is not a race to the finish line. What matters is not how much you do but rather, the quality of the things that you do. As Lao Tzu, the ancient Chinese philosopher and writer, said, "Doing nothing is better than being busy doing nothing."

Start doing more by doing less. Cast aside the guilt and reintroduce yourself to the world around you. Savor life's simple moments. Taste your food rather than gorging it. Listen between the lines rather than hearing words. Reignite relationships rather than passing like visitors in the night. Make a moment rather than counting the minutes. You just might get the BIG idea when you expect it least. And you'll feel more relaxed, less distracted, and blissfully rejuvenated to greet another day. Sometimes you accomplish more by doing less. You DO get something for nothing! :)

"

The only way
an annoyance
can bring you down
is if you let it.

"

COMPLAINING NEVER SOLVED A PROBLEM

Complaining, complaining, complaining. For some people, it's their job. (And they're good at it.) They complain about the weather, the noise level, and their personal comfort. They complain about their job, their kids, and how the world's been unfair to them. In fact, they pretty much complain about everything. If you didn't know better, you'd think they have real problems, but the fact is, they don't. Their biggest problem is that they complain too much.

As Sydney J. Harris, the American journalist, said, "When I hear somebody sigh, 'Life is hard,' I am always tempted to ask, 'Compared to what?' "

WHAT'S THE PROBLEM?

We all have situations that get under our skin, but are they problems? It depends on your view.

It's a *nuisance* when you have to get somewhere and the person in front of you drives slowwwwwly. It's a *pain* when your neighbor wakes you up with his lawn mower or your umbrella breaks in a driving rain. It's an *annoyance* when the restaurant table is sticky, the person in front of you on the plane reclines her seat, or the deer eats all your new plantings. It's *aggravating* when they close a driving lane, your phone autocorrects your text "massage," or you spill ketchup on your new pants.

Although annoyances may be upsetting, the way you react to them is key. The fact is…no one's hurt, the event isn't life changing, and you'll probably forget about it by the end of the day.

Some people, however, view irritations as problems. They allow nuisances to get them into a funk, make them lash out at friends and family, or turn a perfectly good day into a lousy one. The truth is, some people have "real" problems. Be grateful you're not one of them today.

ATTITUDE MAKES ALL THE DIFFERENCE

Do you turn irritations into problems? If so, here are five thoughts worth considering:

Be positive. Some people choose to see clouds on a sunny day. Keep in mind that a positive mental attitude can improve your health, enhance your relationships, increase your chances of success, and add years to your life. So view the glass as half-full rather than half empty.

Be realistic. If you expect miracles, you're bound to let yourself down. The key is to set ambitious, yet realistic expectations. The philosopher Voltaire warned against letting the perfect be the enemy of the good. That advice still holds true today.

Be mindful. Some things are beyond your control. If you can't change a situation, change the way you look at it. The fact is, life is filled with "ups and downs," so make the most of the "in-betweens."

Let it go. Don't dwell on nuisances. If you have to blow off steam, count to 10 and move on. The only way an annoyance can bring you down is if you let it.

Keep things in perspective. Don't let a minor inconvenience ruin your whole day. Remember the difference between an annoyance and a problem.

YOU CAN'T CHANGE THE WEATHER

Things happen. Your cable provider places you on hold, your car needs repairs, your Internet goes down (ugh). Get over it. You can't change the weather, and it's hard to change people if they're not willing participants. So next time you're confronted by an inconvenience, remember…life goes on. Don't let a minor hassle affect your mood or interrupt the flow of your day. Negative thinking will get you down, and complaining will only make matters worse.

As Maya Angelou, the Pulitzer Prize-nominated poet, said, "You may not control all the events that happen to you, but you can decide not to be reduced by them." So the next time a car cuts you off, the store runs out of your favorite ice cream, or someone nearby shouts on his cell phone, remember to think, "No problem." **:)**

Being frugal doesn't mean slashing your spending or depriving yourself of things that you enjoy. It means knowing the value of a dollar and making every effort to spend it wisely.

14 PRICELESS STRATEGIES FOR BEING FRUGAL

When some people go on a diet, they "starve" themselves until they reach their desired weight. It's only natural that when the same people look for ways to be frugal, they try to cut their budget to shreds. The truth is, just as it pays to adopt a healthy lifestyle for weight control, the same commonsense approach applies to frugality.

14 TIME-TESTED TIPS TO SAVE MONEY

Cheaper isn't always less expensive. Some folks compare the price of products without factoring workmanship or product life into the equation. As a result, they end up paying more for several things of *inferior* quality than for one thing of *high* quality. Remember, it's less expensive to buy good quality up front — think "one and done."

Hidden costs are visible. The true cost of a purchase isn't always visible. For example, when you buy a new computer, consider the cost of downtime, lost productivity learning the new system, and even software upgrades that may be required. Remember, hidden costs may be invisible to your eye, but they're very visible to your wallet.

A penny can cost you dollars. Sometimes the effort required to save a few pennies far exceeds the benefit. (For example, driving miles out of your way to save a few cents on gasoline.) Remember, if you spend less time trying to save pennies, you'll have more time to make dollars.

New doesn't make it better. Some folks buy things simply because they're new. The question is, "Does the new product offer *significantly* greater benefits than the existing one?" If not, don't buy the hype. Remember to think before you jump.

Saving can cost you dearly. Some folks bet that the likelihood of a catastrophe is so small that protection isn't required. While that may save money in the short term, they're gambling that a fire, flood, lawsuit, or illness won't devastate them. Remember to protect your downside — unless you're willing to lose it all.

Pay now or pay later. Think twice before trying to save money on an attorney, tax professional, or financial advisor. Experienced professionals often provide benefits that exceed their fee. Remember that just because you're *able to do something* doesn't mean you should.

Thanks for nothing. Some folks fail to consider the *cost of money* during the buying process. When you finance a purchase, the interest you pay over the term of the loan doesn't provide any benefit. Remember, if you don't have the money, don't spend it.

You can't cut your way to wealth. Some folks spend too much time trying to *cut costs* and too little time *investing* their money. Remember to invest your savings wisely, and you'll earn money in your sleep.

Pass up this opportunity. Some folks are actually *more* interested in buying something because it's on sale than they are in owning it. Remember, if you don't need something, any sales price is too high.

Pay up for that familiar name. Some folks think that name-brand merchandise is superior to private label because the name sounds familiar. Remember, when you buy a name brand you're also paying for its advertising.

Think no-brainer. There are many ways to be frugal without sacrificing anything. For example, walk instead of taking a taxi; watch movies on streaming TV instead of always at the theater; brown-bag your lunch instead of going out. Remember, inexpensive pleasures are still pleasures.

Shop value rather than price. Some folks use cost as the only criterion for a purchase. That's unwise because products and services are rarely the same. Consider such things as the seller's reputation, the quality of its goods, and the organization's willingness to stand behind its product. Remember, you get what you pay for.

An ounce of prevention. Some folks skimp on preventive maintenance to save money. They put off changing the oil in their car; they delay getting their house gutters cleaned; or they avoid going to the dentist for routine checkups. Remember to maintain your things today or they may come back to bite you tomorrow.

Waste not, want not. There are many simple ways to stop wasting money. For example, some folks open credit card accounts to get store discounts, but they pay off the balance slowly, adding interest and possibly late fees. Other people run into a store without feeding the parking meter, only to find a parking ticket on the windshield when they return. (Ouch!) Last, some people maintain gym memberships or keep magazine subscriptions active even if they don't use or read them. Remember to plug the holes before filling the bucket.

GET MORE FOR YOUR MONEY

Being frugal doesn't mean slashing your spending or depriving yourself of things that you enjoy. It means knowing the value of a dollar and making every effort to spend it wisely.

Let's keep frugality in perspective. We can spend so much time scrutinizing our habits and worrying about money that it becomes all-consuming. While saving is a virtue, moderation is the balance of life. Remember, your money's not worth anything if you don't spend it — but spend and invest it wisely! **:)**

People who are frugal understand the value of a dollar and make informed and thoughtful decisions. People who are cheap try to spend as little money as possible.

ARE YOU CHEAP OR FRUGAL?

Saving money is an admirable goal, but like anything else in life, it can be taken to the extreme. The truth is, there's a BIG difference between being frugal and being cheap. Frugality is a virtue; being cheap is not.

People who are frugal understand the value of a dollar and make informed and thoughtful decisions. People who are cheap try to spend as little money as possible. Period. While frugal people buy value, cheap people shop price.

Here are nine ways that frugal people distinguish themselves from cheapskates.

LIVING "ON THE CHEAP"

Cheap people sacrifice quality for price. Frugal people are always on the hunt for value and are willing to pay up when they find it. Cheap people only care about price.

Cheap people can be selfish. Frugal people are thrifty with themselves but generous to others. Cheap people have been known to order an expensive meal and then shortchange their friends when the bill is divided. They've also been known to dine out at an expensive restaurant and then stiff the waiter to save money.

Cheap people bend the rules. Frugal people rarely pass up a good deal. Cheap people, on the other hand, go to extremes to save money — even if it's shady. For example, cheap people have been known to lie about their age to receive a discount, to borrow something with no intention of returning it, or to wear clothes and then return them as new.

Cheap people hoard their money. Frugal people think twice before buying something new. Cheap people try to run something into the ground, and then some, before opening their wallet.

Cheap people are penny-wise and pound-foolish. Frugal people measure the true cost of a purchase. (This includes the value of time as well as the maintenance and repair costs over the life of the product.) Cheap people can't see the forest for the trees. In fact, they'd consider traveling miles out of their way to save a few pennies on gasoline.

Cheap people are obsessed with saving money. Frugal people try to be economical. Cheap people go to any length to save a few pennies. For example, cheap people may gain more pleasure from saving money than from enjoying a night out with friends. You'll also find cheapskates bringing ketchup home from a fast-food restaurant or serving food that's long past its expiration date.

Cheap people skimp on important necessities. Frugal people spend money wisely on things they consider a priority. Cheap folks put off a doctor/dentist visit, even when they feel miserable.

Cheap people pressure others for discounts. Frugal people understand that everyone has the right to earn a living. Cheap people are never embarrassed to haggle over price.

Cheap people buy things because they're cheap. Frugal people buy things they need. Cheap people buy something simply because it's on sale — regardless of whether they want or need it.

YOU GET WHAT YOU PAY FOR

Money is a funny thing. Some people view it as a measure of their self-worth, while others view money as a necessary evil. For some people, money is a blessing, while for others, it's a curse. The key is to keep a healthy view of money. Consider the following:

Keep money in perspective. Some folks spend so much time worrying about money that parting with it diminishes the joy of making any purchase or appreciating the moment.

Avoid viewing shopping as a sport. Don't treat shopping as a competition where winning — getting an amazing deal — gives you more pleasure than owning the merchandise.

Be conscious of your spending habits. Focus the bulk of your purchases on what you *need* rather than on what you *want*.

Spend money on priorities. Money is worth something only if you spend it. Therefore, spend it on things that are *most* important to you.

Make sure your decisions add up. Think big picture. If you're moving heaven and earth to save a few pennies a year, but you're making yourself a nervous wreck, get a life.

Saving can be costly. Cheapskates can damage their relationships with others by their behavior. Determine the impact that your decisions have on those around you.

Manage your money. Earning money is only a start. Grow your money by saving/investing it properly, so that you make money while you sleep. Remember, you can't cut your way to wealth.

Don't spend what you don't have. As Will Rogers said, "Too many people spend money they haven't earned to buy things they don't want to impress people they don't like."

Money should be a means to support yourself and your family. It should never become the cornerstone of your life or define you as a person. Unfortunately, some people let money consume them and take on a role larger than life. That's neither sensible nor healthy. Frugality is smart. It compels you to live within your means, make informed and thoughtful decisions, appreciate all the things that money *can't* buy, and best of all — frugality buys you a good night's sleep. As the saying goes, "If you want to be richer, make more money or need less." **:)**

It's better to bite your tongue than eat your words.

MAY I HAVE A
WORD WITH YOU?

While it takes only a few words to make someone feel really special, words poorly chosen have the power to destroy a valuable relationship, tarnish a reputation, or become the cause of endless embarrassment.

Yet in today's fast-paced world with its cryptic, sound-bite mentality, we're more likely to sacrifice sensitivity for speed, and quality for quantity. This leaves our listeners to sort out for themselves the consequences of our ill-considered remarks.

WORDS OF APOLOGY

"I'm sorry." When did the phrase "I'm sorry" morph into "I'm sorry, but..."? If you're sincerely sorry, then apologize, without reservation. If you're not sorry, skip the apology and avoid compounding the problem.

"I made a mistake." "I was wrong." How many times do people apologize, only to repeat the act again later? It's as though we apologize without realizing that our apology is an implied promise not to make the mistake again.

Eat your words. Did you ever let words slip off your tongue without realizing the consequences? Sometimes a little discretion can save you from a very embarrassing situation. The fact is, it's better to bite your tongue than eat your words.

WORDS OF ACKNOWLEDGMENT

"Please" and "Thank you." While it doesn't take much effort to say "Please" and "Thank you," some people forgo these pleasantries because they don't know better, while others apparently feel these words are beneath their "pay grade." How much effort does it take to thank someone for a job well done?

WORDS OF HONOR

"I promise." "Trust me." Whenever you say "Trust me" to someone, you imply that you're worthy of his or her trust. Some people, however, think that breaking a small promise doesn't count. The fact is, the words "I promise" and "Trust me" put your honor on the line. Don't use them if you don't mean them.

"Can you do me a favor?" Stop and think before you ask someone to do you a favor. Is your request reasonable? Are you putting a friend in an uncomfortable position? Are you becoming too reliant on the same individual? Inappropriate requests destroy relationships.

A play on words. Twisting words, dancing around the truth, or telling a "white lie" produces the same result — the loss of trust and credibility. Excuses such as "Everybody does it," "It was only a white lie," or "I only stretched a few small details" don't cut it. Once you misrepresent the truth, everything you say in the future may be suspect.

FIGHTING WORDS

Spread the word. Gossip is a disease spread by word of mouth. If you're saying something behind someone's back, it's only a matter of time before you're saying it behind mine. Nothing more need be said.

"I HATE you!" Some people hit with fists, others with words. Be careful where you point your mouth.

WORDS OF WISDOM: LESSONS TO BE LEARNED

At a loss for words? Some people avoid personal confrontation at all costs, while others feel sheepish telling someone how much they really care. People aren't mind readers. If you fail to say what's on your mind, you may regret it once you've lost the opportunity — perhaps forever.

Words are permanent. Once words leave your mouth, they are impossible to retract. Words stand the test of time. For example, the Bill of Rights (a mere 462 words) has served as our country's beacon since 1789.

@#%^%*?%! Just because you're mouthing words doesn't mean that you're saying something. Some people use jargon to impress their friends and colleagues. You may as well be talking to yourself. Actually, you are.

Actions speak louder than words. Saying something doesn't make it so. Sayings such as "Practice what you preach," "Talk is cheap," "Talk a good game," and "Walk the talk" all say the same thing — that your actions will either confirm or contradict your words.

Remember, effective communication requires more than choosing your words carefully. Words, after all, have at least two meanings: what you intend to say and what the listener thinks you said.

MAKE YOUR WORDS COUNT

We have a choice…make a better effort to communicate properly or spend more time doing damage control.

Although we say we don't have time for quality communication, we seem to have all the time in the world for trying to repair a misunderstanding, patch up damaged feelings, mend a wounded relationship, restore a blemished reputation, apologize for shooting off our mouth, or reorganize after working at cross-purposes.

If you're thinking that it's time to slow down because there's too much at stake — you took the words right out of my mouth. **:)**

"

While social media helps us keep in touch with our casual acquaintances, meaningful relationships require something more...

"

THERE'S MORE TO FRIENDSHIP THAN FRIENDING

Your definition of friendship may change during your lifetime, but its value won't. True friends have fun together, even when they're doing nothing special. They communicate without talking and seem close despite living miles apart. True friends take time to listen to your problem when you're having a terrible day and help you find the sun on a stormy day. True friends are a source of honest feedback and continuous support. They watch your back, preserve your innermost secrets, and lend you a shoulder when things go south.

STAGES OF FRIENDSHIP

There are several different stages of a friendship — beginning with casual acquaintance, then meaningful relationship, and finally, lasting friendship. While social media helps us keep in touch with our casual acquaintances, meaningful relationships require something more, while lasting friendships demand still greater personal commitment.

1 Casual Acquaintance
- Fun
- Positive
- Accepting
- Considerate
- Tolerant
- Respectful
- Ethical

2 Meaningful Relationship
- Trustworthy
- Open
- Honest
- Thoughtful
- Fair
- Giving
- Dependable
- Sincere
- Loyal
- Forgiving
- Sharing
- Supportive
- Committed

3 Lasting Friendship
- Authenticity
- Communication
- Selflessness
- Personal Growth
- Faith

THE DEFINING CHARACTERISTICS OF A FRIEND

Casual acquaintance. You probably have a lot of casual acquaintances. You meet them at parties, go to school with them, or live in their neighborhood. You may know their names or recognize their faces. Yet, although you enjoy their company, none of you have invested enough of yourselves to develop meaningful relationships.

As you form a relationship with a casual acquaintance, you may size up him or her to see if that person is *fun, positive, accepting, considerate, tolerant, respectful, and ethical*. And, if you share common interests and stick with it, both of you may make a commitment that takes the friendship to the next level.

Meaningful relationship. In this stage, people gradually commit to a friendship by making small gestures and gauging the other's response. As the friendship develops, each person becomes more invested in and committed to the relationship.

In the process of developing a meaningful relationship, people look for a friend who is *trustworthy, open, honest, thoughtful, fair, giving, dependable, sincere, loyal, forgiving, sharing, supportive,* and *committed*. In addition, they would also expect this friend to possess all the fundamental qualities found in a casual acquaintance.

When consistent behavior is exhibited over time, the relationship becomes predictable. This is the start of a lasting friendship, in which *authenticity, communication, selflessness, personal growth,* and *faith* thrive.

Lasting friendship. Lasting friendships don't happen by chance; they bloom because friends care as much about their friend's happiness as they do their own. As Ralph Waldo Emerson once said, "The only way to have a friend is to be one."

The qualities that lead to deeper, lasting friendships are:

> *Authenticity.* You can always "be yourself" around your friend. There are no games, and there is no need to measure your words or actions. You are accepted and appreciated for being you.

Communication. Your relationship is open and honest. You always tell the truth — even if it hurts. You feel comfortable sharing your life and innermost secrets with your friend.

Selflessness. Your friend wants what's best for you. Period. There's give-and-take in any healthy relationship. There's no need to keep score. You gain considerable pleasure by witnessing your friend's happiness and success.

Personal growth. Your friend brings out the best in you and helps to make you a better person.

Faith. Your friend has your back in good times and bad. You have so much trust and confidence in the relationship that you never have reason to question your friend's motives. As someone once said, "Good friends are like stars. You don't always see them, but you know that they're always there."

FRIENDS FOR LIFE

Are you a good friend? Let's look at some of the telltale signs. A true friend takes action before a request is made; she volunteers to be the designated driver on New Year's Eve; he helps himself to a beer rather than wanting to be "waited on"; she doesn't take the picture because she's expected to be included in the family photo; he doesn't leave the party with the crowd but instead, stays to clean up the mess; when he is awakened by your call, he still says he's so glad to hear from you; she throws you a celebration party even though you beat her out for the promotion; he knows it's only an argument and not the end of the friendship; she loses more sleep over your problems than over her own; he knows you'd give him the shirt off your back, although he'd never ask; she gives you the bigger piece of cake, even if it's chocolate.

Being a friend involves so much more than doing a favor for someone or having an occasional chat on social media. It means more than sharing a sandwich or an occasional smile. Friends are people who share one another's dreams, open their hearts, and complete one another's life. As Muhammad Ali once said, "Friendship...is *not* something you learn in school. But if you haven't learned the meaning of friendship, you really haven't learned anything." **:)**

You may not have
the control to lengthen
your life, but you can
do much to deepen it.

GOOD CONVERSATIONS REQUIRE MORE THAN TALKING

Did you ever spend time with someone and feel as though they weren't there? You may have occupied the same room, but you just didn't connect. Whether this is an isolated occurrence or the hallmark of that relationship, it could be a warning sign of trouble ahead.

Unfortunately, broken relationships don't happen in a vacuum. Many of us unknowingly erect communication barriers, making it difficult for relationships to thrive.

9 WARNING SIGNS OF A CONVERSATION GOING BAD

Communication barriers don't *happen* to us; they're *created* by us. So as easy as it is for us to create them, we can tear them down. Do any of these folks or attitudes sound familiar?

Juggler. Some people are always multitasking. They do so much that you're never really sure if they're merely "hearing" you — or actually listening to what you have to say.

Busy bee. Some folks rush from activity to activity with no time to spare. Good luck pinning them down for a civilized conversation.

Distracted. Some people can't even spell focus, much less practice it. They look at their watch, shout instructions, or pick up the phone while they talk to you.

Daydreamer. Some folks may be physically present, yet their mind is clearly somewhere else. (Huh…did you say something?)

Hard shell. Some people are so guarded that you can't expect more than a trivial conversation. You may know them for years and still call them an acquaintance.

Taskmaster. Some folks reduce you to an item on their to-do list. They call or visit you because they *have to*, not because they *want to* (and it shows).

Intolerant. Some people with personal bias or prejudice "shut down" when certain topics come up. If they don't agree with your position, they may hear you, but they're not really listening.

Game player. Some people make you feel like you're playing *Wheel of Fortune*. They call you from their car and due to bad cell service, all you hear is every fourth word. I guess you're expected to fill in the blanks.

Egotist. Some folks are so busy talking about themselves, they never even consider that you might have something to say. As George Bernard Shaw said, "The trouble with her is that she lacks the power of conversation but not the power of speech."

LOOKING FOR A MEANINGFUL CONVERSATION?

Here are 10 activities that'll help strengthen conversations and enhance relationships:

Buy some breathing room. When an agenda is packed too tight, there's a tendency to spend more time focusing on your schedule than on the moment. The best way to combat overscheduling is by saying *no* to low-priority items so that you can say *yes* to high-priority ones.

Avoid distractions. Give your undivided attention to the person you're with. Put down your phone. Stop looking at the clock. Yes…the to-do list can wait.

Choose your location wisely. It's difficult to have a productive conversation in a loud restaurant or bar. So choose a place that's conducive to discussion.

Make the person feel special. Be genuine. Make eye contact. Make the person feel like he or she is the only one who matters (at least for that moment).

Turn off the television. If you're looking for quality time, watching TV together hinders conversation. You may know a lot about the program but little about what's happening in his or her life.

Keep a level head. A few drinks make great company. After a few more, you probably won't have a meaningful conversation, much less remember what you talked about.

Never respond emotionally. If you're angry or upset, count to 10 before communicating your feelings. If that doesn't work, try 20.

Be genuine and truthful. Honesty is a critical ingredient of a trusting relationship. It's important to tell it like it is, rather than placate people by telling them what they want to hear.

Show that you care. Make sure you don't dominate the conversation. Listen actively rather than thinking about your response. Be empathetic. Put yourself in their shoes. Read between the lines. Speak slowly, in language they'll understand. Validate your understanding of what you discussed.

Get the signal. If you're "visiting" someone via cell phone, make sure you have a strong signal. And don't surf the web during the conversation.

BEING PRESENT IS NOT THE SAME AS BEING THERE

In an effort to accomplish more, we multitask, overcommit ourselves, and try to squeeze as much as we can into the day. The result is that by choosing quantity over quality, we end up compromising something very special — meaningful conversations. Is that what you want?

Sometimes life's biggest challenges are best addressed by going back to basics. In this case, that means focusing, listening, and caring. While the world is moving at light speed, slowing down may actually increase your productivity and make life more rewarding. Meaningful conversations are the linchpin of any successful relationship. You may not have the control to lengthen your life, but you can do much to deepen it. Good conversations require more than talking. **:)**

"

Failing one time —
or even several times
— doesn't make you
a failure any more than
losing one game
makes you a loser.

"

FAILING DOESN'T MAKE YOU A FAILURE

You blew the test, you lost the game, and you made a complete fool out of yourself in front of everyone. (Ouch.) But worst of all, you're beginning to doubt yourself, and you're starting to view yourself as a failure. Please don't do that! Failing one time — or even several times — doesn't make you a failure any more than losing one game makes you a loser. Believing you're a failure, however, can make you act like a failure and that can become a self-fulfilling prophecy.

Failing comes in three flavors. First, despite our best efforts, there's nothing that you can do to prevent *accidents*, as they are by their very nature out of your control. Second, everyone makes *mistakes*, such as poor choices or misjudgments…no one's perfect. The third type of failures — *errors* — is preventable. They're caused by carelessness, inaccuracy, or poor judgment. For the most part, people are very forgiving if you make an honest mistake or act out of character on occasion. But when improper actions — such as lying, cheating, or stealing — are repeated or intentional, your reputation suffers. Even if you offer a heartfelt apology after a transgression, it can still take considerable time and effort to recover.

HOW SHOULD YOU REACT TO FAILURE?

Be realistic. If you demand perfection of yourself, you're setting yourself up for disappointment.

Don't take failure personally. Making a mistake doesn't make you a failure. It's simply a reminder that you're human.

Accept responsibility. Nothing positive is ever gained by scapegoating. Be courageous and accept responsibility for your failure.

Be nice to yourself. Don't tear yourself down for failing. You don't speak to others that way, so give yourself a break.

Get back on the horse. Don't wallow in self-pity. Obsessing over failure won't make it better. You cannot change the past, but you can affect the future.

Grow from your mistakes. Take the time to reflect on your experience, learn from your mistakes, and adapt accordingly.

Don't quit. Most people fail before achieving success; the difference is that successful people never stop trying. As Douglas MacArthur said, "Age wrinkles the body. Quitting wrinkles the soul."

IF ALL ELSE FAILS

Failing should be viewed as a hurdle rather than a roadblock. Successful people aren't discouraged by failure. They know that every worthwhile goal carries some element of disappointment. Failure is a challenge to be overcome, a test to defy your will, and in the end, a learning opportunity. For others, failure is viewed negatively as an opportunity to feel sorry and complain, a reason to belittle oneself, and an excuse to give up too quickly.

The fact is, it's important to remember that most successful people fail BIG TIME before reaching the pinnacle of success. According to Business Insider.com:

> Thomas Edison's teachers told him he was "too stupid to learn anything." Walt Disney was fired by a newspaper editor because he "lacked imagination and had no good ideas." In one of Fred Astaire's first screen tests, an executive wrote: "Can't sing. Can't act. Slightly balding. Can dance a little." Charles Darwin was considered an average student. He gave up on a career in medicine and was going to school to become a parson. Vincent Van Gogh sold only one painting, *The Red Vineyard*, in his life, and the sale was just months before his death. Lucille Ball appeared in so many second-tier films at the start of her career that she became known as "The Queen of B Movies." Theodor Seuss Geisel, better known as Dr. Seuss, had his first book rejected by 27 different publishers. J.K. Rowling was a single mom living off welfare when she began writing the first Harry Potter novel. Rowling is now internationally renowned for her seven-book Harry Potter series and, in U.S. currency, became the first billionaire author in 2004.*

The bottom line is that there's still some hope for the rest of us.

The truth is, the difference between a stepping-stone and a stumbling block is the way in which you approach it. Failing can be a blessing or a curse. It can be a great teacher, make you stronger, and keep you grounded, or it can be the cause of your demise. It's your choice. Your view of failure determines your reality. As Zig Ziglar said, "Remember that failure is an event, not a person." You're not a failure unless you make yourself one. **:)**

*Source: http://www.businessinsider.com/successful-people-who-failed-at-first-2014-3

Appreciate what
you have, while you
have it, or you'll learn
what it meant to you
after you lose it.

DO YOU TAKE IT FOR GRANTED?

Are you grateful for the life that you have? Or do you take things for granted? Maybe you haven't thought about it for a while. Did you ever fail to appreciate someone you care about? Was that because you were too busy putting out fires or focusing on other things? Or perhaps you assumed they'd just hang around forever.

The problem is, when you take people or things for granted, you put them in jeopardy. It's not enough to make up for neglect after they've slipped away. It's important to be grateful every day for the wonderful things in your life. Think of this as a wake-up call.

WHAT DO YOU TAKE FOR GRANTED?

Choices. We marry the love of our life, pursue the career of our dreams, and vote for the candidate of our choice. Free choice, however, is not a given everywhere.

Loyalty. People remain faithful to us through good times and bad. When was the last time you showed your appreciation?

Customers. We have customers who've been with us for years. Do you appreciate their loyalty as much today as when you were chasing their business?

Health. We don't appreciate good health until we feel lousy. When we get better, we take our health for granted again. (So much for learning from our mistakes.)

Freedom. We have: the right to privacy, the freedom to speak our mind, and the privilege to practice the religion of our choice. It wasn't always that way. People gave their lives to protect those freedoms.

Love of your life. Your spouse may be the most important person in your life. Do you take his or her love for granted?

Variety. We have so many travel options, food choices, and retail alternatives available to us. Not everyone has that luxury.

Trust. Your faith in those who are close to you enables you to share your deepest secrets with them. Do you realize how special that trust is?

Dedicated employees. We have employees who do everything we ask of them — and more. Do you acknowledge their value — or take it for granted?

Parents. You have parents who offer their unconditional love. They've given a lot of themselves to ensure that you have a better life. Show some gratitude. If you're not one already, you'll probably be a parent one day.

Security. We have reasonable weather, access to healthy food, and can walk the streets safely at night. Be thankful that we don't live in fear.

Basic necessities. We have three meals a day, a warm bed to sleep in, and a shelter over our head. To some people, that's a luxury.

Nature. After days of bad weather, we appreciate the sunshine. Maybe we shouldn't take clean air or water for granted.

Life. Every day is a gift. Do you take that for granted?

APPRECIATE WHAT YOU HAVE
BEFORE IT BECOMES WHAT YOU HAD

One day we should take a moment and listen to ourselves. We complain about not having *enough* while we lose sight of the wonderful things that we have. That happens because we get restless, things become too routine, or perhaps because we enjoy the hunt for something new.

The problem is, when we take stuff for granted, things eventually go south…the relationship goes sour, the employee jumps ship, the customer goes to a competitor. And, of course — then we react with panic. So don't take things for granted. Appreciate what you have, while you have it, or you'll learn what it meant to you after you lose it. **:)**

Don't wait a lifetime to satisfy your needs or you may live to regret it one day.

HAVE-TO VS. WANT-TO

Ever hear a person approaching retirement say, "Now I'm going to start doing what I *want* to do — not what I *have* to do"? It got me thinking. How much time do we spend doing what is expected of us rather than what we really want to do?

Unfortunately, we do what we "have to" do all too often. We dress up for dinner even though we'd rather go casual; we stay after hours to impress the boss; we go to the annual party, yet again, even though it was boring last year. You get my drift?

Before you know it, one simple gesture becomes habit, and you find yourself spending a lifetime doing things for reasons other than because *you* want to.

LIFE IS DEMANDING

Here are seven reasons why we feel compelled to give in to demands that are placed on us:

Satisfaction. Most of us want to please those we hold in high regard. So we do "what we have to" to satisfy family members, friends, and superiors.

Acceptance. When we're young, we want to be friends with the cool kids. When we're older, we do "what we have to" to become "members" of groups that we admire.

Acknowledgment. All of us prefer a pat on the back rather than an ugly frown from others. So we adjust our behavior to win praise.

Reward. We "kiss up" to folks who can benefit us personally. We do "what we have to" to secure that reward or promotion.

Fear. We simply do "what we have to" to avoid criticism or punishment.

Payback. We feel a responsibility to pay back those who've done things for us in the past.

Conformity. We do "what we have to" to conform to expected norms rather than stand out in the crowd.

ARE YOUR HAVE-TO'S OVERWHELMING YOU?

Are expectations real or imagined? Do people make you feel obligated to satisfy their expectations or are you putting pressure on yourself?

How hard do you try to gain acceptance? It takes a lot of energy to masquerade as someone else. In fact, it's exhausting. Real friends accept you for who you are, not who they want you to be.

Do you compromise your principles to please others? Listen to your conscience. If you're not ready to do something, don't let others convince you that you are. Remember, you have to live with yourself for the rest of your life.

Do friends and family expect payback for their support? Real friends don't keep score. They give of themselves without expecting something in return.

How much time do you spend trying to look good? Great organizations reward people based on performance rather than politics. Every minute that you spend promoting yourself is valuable time you could be doing something worthwhile.

Are you being asked to give more than you can? If you give generously of yourself, don't let others make you feel guilty. To some people, enough is never enough. People can make you feel guilty *only* if you allow them to.

Are your expectations of yourself unreasonable? Some people are perfectionists; they always want to give more. The problem is that they're tough on themselves to a fault. Do what you can. You're only human.

DO IT FOR YOU

There's a very fine line between trying to please others so much that your own needs aren't being met. This creates a tug-of-war with no "right" answer — but we're continually forced to make one anyway. As W. Clement Stone, the inspirational author, said, "You always do what you want to do. This is true with every act. You may say that you had to do something, or that you were forced to, but actually, whatever you do, you do by choice. Only you have the power to choose for yourself." So how do you choose? Solving this dilemma begins by knowing your personal values, establishing priorities, managing other people's expectations, and yes…believing in yourself.

When you believe in yourself, you'll be proud of who you are rather than pretending to be who others want you to be; you'll pursue what you love most rather than being hijacked by the needs of others; you'll strive for the standards that you set for yourself rather than seeking the approval and validation of others. And you'll know in your heart that you've given what you can while managing to reserve some for yourself.

Satisfying your own needs does not make you a bad person. In fact, it enables you to share your happiness with people closest to you and still have enough to give a smile away to a stranger in need. Don't wait a lifetime to satisfy your needs or you may live to regret it one day. As George Bernard Shaw, the Irish playwright, said, "Take care to get what you like or you will be forced to like what you get." Don't do this because you have to. Do it because you want to! **:)**

"

Although the costs
of not delegating may
be invisible, the price
that you pay is real.

"

ATTENTION, CONTROL FREAKS: IT'S TIME TO DELEGATE

You're smart, you're gifted, and you're self-assured. You dot your "i's," you cross your "t's," and you've got pride and a work ethic that's second to none. In fact, when you put your mind to something, your work is always outstanding. So I completely understand why you believe "the only way to get things done right is to do them myself." BUT…if you're a control freak, and prefer not to delegate, you may be hurting yourself in ways you've never imagined.

It's a fallacy to think that being a control freak provides the best outcome. The reality is, although the costs of not delegating may be invisible, the price that you pay is real.

IT PAYS TO DELEGATE

Increase your value. What portion of your workday is spent doing high-level versus routine activities? If you spend significant time doing tedious work, when you're capable of more, you're not doing yourself any favors.

Grow your *service* business. As you grow your business, you'll reach a point where there aren't enough hours in the day to serve your clients alone. If you don't "clone" yourself, your clients have the choice of waiting in line for you or going to a competitor.

Get a life. You're so good at your job that people have become dependent on you. Before you know it, you're working evenings and weekends to keep everyone happy. If you don't off-load some work, there'll come a time when you'll resent your job.

Increase family time. Why hire a contractor if you can do the work yourself, right? The truth is, while you may be saving money, your loss of quality time with your family is a high price to pay.

Gain expertise. With today's software, it's easy to prepare your own taxes. The problem is, with laws constantly changing you may be overlooking something that costs you dearly. The fact is, even though you're able to do something doesn't mean you should do it. Sometimes it makes sense to hire a professional.

Boost your career. Some folks believe that making themselves indispensable enhances their career. So, with an eye on a promotion, they hoard information and keep everything close to the vest. The problem is, with no one able to fill their role, they're creating a significant barrier to their own advancement.

Leverage your talent. As you work your way up the ladder, your performance is measured more by what gets accomplished than by what *you* personally do. So don't try to do everything yourself. Instead, hire great people, train them well, inspire them, and get out of their way.

IT'S TIME TO LET GO

Here are 10 rules worth considering:

Leave your comfort zone. If you don't feel comfortable delegating, you're not alone. Change is difficult. Think about it this way…if we didn't try to walk, we'd all still be crawling.

Know what matters most. Set priorities and determine which trade-offs are right for you.

Build trust. Surround yourself with talented people who possess a high level of trust and integrity.

Manage the process. Focus on the process as much as on the end result. And make sure to consider strengths and weaknesses when assigning work.

Be explicit about goals and expectations. Tell people your ultimate goal rather than micromanaging how they do it. Who knows…they may come up with a better way.

Set milestones. Delegating does *not* mean walking away from an activity until it's complete. Establish key milestones and review progress along the way.

Delegate responsibility *and* authority. It's not enough to delegate a task. Give the person the responsibility and authority to get it done.

Set the right tone. Create an environment in which dialog is open, questions are encouraged, and mistakes become part of a learning experience.

Give continual feedback. Remember, there's a difference between criticism and constructive feedback.

Recognize and reward excellence. Give credit where credit is due. Compliment people in public; criticize them in private.

BEING IN CONTROL IS AN ILLUSION

When was the last time you questioned whether being a control freak makes sense? On the one hand, control freaks are motivated by the thought of achieving perfection, and on the other hand, by the fear of letting go. By attempting to control everything, however, the only thing control freaks guarantee is the potential to drive themselves crazy, and in the process, to lose quality family time, to perform inferior work compared to an "expert," to limit the size of their business, or to damage their chance for a promotion. All of that in the name of perfection!

We can't control fate, the weather, or the height of our kids. And believe it or not, the sun continues to rise and set every day without our help. So, whether you're a parent, boss, or do-it-yourselfer, maybe it's time to have some faith in other people — and delegate. Who knows…if you surround yourself with great people, you'll probably get great results. As the saying goes, "You may not be able to control every situation and its outcome, but you can control your attitude and how you deal with it." It's time to delegate. **:)**

Take ownership
of your life decisions
rather than relinquishing
that responsibility
to others.

DON'T FEEL GUILTY...JUST SAY "NO"!

Are you the type of person who feels guilty saying "no"? Sure…it's easy to bow to everyone's wishes, say "yes" to their requests for help, or follow the crowd. But you're not doing yourself any favors by avoiding the forbidden word. In fact, there *are* definite times when saying "yes" is a no-no.

Every choice you make is like a seesaw, whereby saying "yes" to one thing results in forgoing something else. For example, if you're helping someone address his or her priorities, you're not tending to your own. That's fine *if* you're conscious of the costs and comfortable with the consequences of your decision, but many people don't focus on the price that they pay. Here are twelve trade-offs that we face each day. Is "no" in your vocabulary?

ARE YOU A YES-MAN (OR WOMAN)?

Focus. If you try to be good at everything, you'll end up being mediocre at everything. So be careful to choose where you want to excel.

Resource allocation. Spending time and money on unimportant stuff often forces you to say "no" to things that matter. So concentrate your resources rather than making across-the-board decisions.

Priorities. When you're hijacked by other people's priorities, you don't have time to tackle your own. So make *your* priorities a priority.

Self-respect. When you constantly seek approval, you give more weight to another person's opinion than to your own. So take ownership of your life decisions rather than relinquishing that responsibility to others.

Balance. When you're constantly on the run, you don't have time to smell the roses. So don't try to fill your calendar each day. Happiness is a result of balance rather than intensity.

Personal values. When you succumb to peer pressure, you may live to regret your actions. So hold firm to your beliefs and values.

Happiness. When you spend more time doing *have-to's* rather than want-to's, other people's happiness becomes more important than your own. So make it a habit to say "no" every once in a while — before you become resentful.

Attitude. When you allow negative and unethical people to pollute your thoughts, you're forced to carry a heavy load. So carefully choose the people with whom you associate.

Productivity. Just because some people waste *their* time doesn't entitle them to waste yours. So know when to pass.

Shortcuts. Get-rich-quick schemes rarely pan out in the long run. So don't allow yourself to be talked into every harebrained idea.

Appetite. If you always focus on what you don't have, you'll never be satisfied. So be grateful for the things you do have in your life and stop being obsessed with more.

Conscience. Never let anyone tempt you to compromise your integrity. So listen to your conscience. That's why you have one.

The bottom line is that saying "NO" is a no-brainer!

SAY YES TO NO

Some people feel that saying "yes" is kind, polite, and fair. Others feel it's easy, less confrontational, or that they're following the path of least resistance.

The reality, however, may be contrary to conventional wisdom. Just think...you have time for everyone, except the people you care for most; you have to stay late because you were helping everyone else do their work; you try to keep everyone happy, even though it's making *you* miserable; you agree to go out every night, even though you're close to exhaustion. No. ... Enough!

I know you want to be kind. I know you don't want to let people down. But think about the consequences. What do you gain by making time for others, but none for yourself; becoming wildly successful, but having no time to enjoy it; listening to other's opinions, but rarely your own; working your heart out, but having nothing to show for it; following the crowd, but then feeling guilty for lowering your standards. Does that sound reasonable? "NO WAY," you say! So then — know when to say "no," and begin saying it. **:)**

"

If we disregard our values, we'll open our eyes one day and won't be able to recognize 'our world' anymore.

"

7 REASONS WHY TRADITIONS ARE SO IMPORTANT

When you hear the word holiday, what comes to mind? If you're like most people, shopping, parties, sales, and catalogs rank near the top of your list. The truth is, many holidays are becoming so commercialized that our proud traditions are in danger of becoming trivialized.

Many of us can't even remember the true meaning of the holidays. Memorial Day has morphed from remembering our fallen soldiers to the unofficial beginning of summer. Labor Day's role in recognizing the achievements of organized labor now just marks the end of summer and a return to school. Veterans Day is honored as a day off from work.

Traditions represent a critical piece of our culture. They help form the structure and foundation of our families and our society. They remind us that we are part of a history that defines our past, shapes who we are today and who we are likely to become. Once we ignore the meaning of our traditions, we're in danger of damaging the underpinning of our identity.

- Tradition contributes a sense of comfort and belonging. It brings families together and enables people to reconnect with friends.

- Tradition reinforces values such as freedom, faith, integrity, a good education, personal responsibility, a strong work ethic, and the value of being selfless.

- Tradition provides a forum to showcase role models and celebrate the things that really matter in life.

- Tradition offers a chance to say "thank you" for the contribution that someone has made.

- Tradition enables us to showcase the principles of our Founding Fathers, celebrate diversity, and unite as a country.

- Tradition serves as an avenue for creating lasting memories for our families and friends.

- Tradition offers an excellent context for meaningful pause and reflection.

As leaders, role models, and parents, we must strive to utilize every opportunity available to us to reinforce the values and beliefs that we hold dear. The alternative to action is taking these values for granted. The result is that our beliefs will get so diluted, over time, that our way of life will become foreign to us. It's like good health. You may take it for granted until you lose it. If we disregard our values, we'll open our eyes one day and won't be able to recognize "our world" anymore. The values that support the backbone of our country, our family, and our faith will have drifted for so long that the fabric of our society will be torn.

Don't let thoughtless apathy overshadow tradition. We all have a moral obligation to regularly remind the world why our values matter to us. Laws and regulations won't protect our culture. In fact, somebody recently figured out that we have concocted 35 million laws to enforce the Ten Commandments. So the next time you celebrate a holiday, remember that your real gift and responsibility is to mark the true meaning of the day. Cheers! **:)**

"

If you look into the
mirror and don't like
what you see…don't
blame the mirror.

"

THE BLAME GAME

When our kids were young, they'd run around the house and hurt themselves by accidentally running into a chair. So we played the "blame game" and put the blame on the chair:

> "Ouch. That hurt! Why did you get in my way? We were having so much fun until YOU spoiled it all. Who do you think you are? You're bigger and stronger,…and you hurt me. You're a bully. Why don't you pick on someone your own size?"

And with that, we let our kids hit the chair to show it who was the boss. "Bad, bad chair!"

For some reason, scolding the chair made it all better. (Of course, it's so much easier to blame the chair than to admit fault.) And the kids continued playing.

Although you may think this is a kid's game, some people continue to play the blame game as adults.

> "Don't blame me that I'm out of shape."

> "It's not my fault that I accumulated all this debt."

> "He told me to do it."

I can hear the chorus now, "Bad, bad chair!"

IT'S EASY TO BLAME OTHERS

You have a choice: You can blame shortcomings on the weather, a bad horoscope, or that it's a leap year. Or you can get serious. The truth is, when folks deflect responsibility and cast blame, it serves as nothing more than a crutch and an excuse to stop trying to better themselves. Worse yet, people who continually make excuses why they *can't* succeed convince themselves that failure is inevitable. This causes them to lose faith in themselves and their abilities — and to make it a self-fulfilling prophecy. So be careful how you speak to others because you're probably listening, too.

Successful people, on the other hand, don't blame the world when they fail to achieve something. They accept personal responsibility, learn from their mistakes, and then do something about it. They also know that being unwilling to make the effort is a losing game. In fact, those who say, "I can't" and "I don't want to" trigger the same results.

It is important to note — even though you may be making an effort *today*, you may be paying a price for years of neglect. But that shouldn't deter you from making the effort *now*. The truth is, it takes many years to become an overnight success.

The bottom line is, if you want to achieve something in life, get to work. Things don't happen magically. YOU have to make things happen. So be positive. Stay focused. And remain determined. If you look into the mirror and don't like what you see…don't blame the mirror. Successful people accept responsibility for their destiny; losers play the blame game. **:)**

Dependency purges people of their dreams, makes their spirit atrophy, and enslaves them to a lifetime of mediocrity.

10 WAYS HELPING PEOPLE ONLY MAKES THEM HELPLESS

Sometimes, well-intentioned plans have unintended consequences. Even though our efforts may help the recipients in the short term, we are making them dependent on our good graces, rather than preparing them to accept personal responsibility for their future.

Here are ten examples where helping people only makes them helpless.

Nonsensical no-bids. Some organizations offer sole-source contracts to a company rather than requiring a fair and competitive bidding process. This makes the supplier complacent and dependent, over time, never having had to win the business.

Guaranteed gratuities. Restaurant servers receive a 10%–20% tip, regardless of the service they provide. This teaches servers that halfhearted work still gets a reward. So why try harder? Their complacency ultimately hurts the restaurant because a superior customer experience is built on the establishment's ambiance, food, and service.

Automatic rewards. Annual bonuses are sometimes based on employee tenure or "just showing up" rather than on merit. If high performers receive the same rewards as mediocre employees, then we shouldn't be surprised by complacency and apathy.

Gifts of graduation. Students are promoted to the next grade level regardless of whether they've met the minimum requirements. This "easy path" through school is sure to catch up with the students one day.

"Yes" — the most common cop-out. When we say "yes" to kids merely to placate them, or to avoid a scene in public, they never learn the difference between right and wrong. Saying "no" to your children, when appropriate, is an act of love.

Unqualified quotas. If opportunity is provided to an individual based on special quotas rather than on his or her true qualifications, will this person use quotas as a crutch throughout life?

Questionable *quid pro quos*. Special favors doled out through nepotism or a *quid pro quo* rather than through earning a seat at the table have a real downside. Although the recipients of these favors may make it to the front of the line, the question remains whether they're up to the job.

Mediocre meritocracy. Some organizations fail to counsel mediocre performers. Mistakes ultimately become poor habits. Allowing employees to "get by" in this way helps neither the employees nor the organization.

Emotional excuses. Often, appeals are issued that encourage people to buy from a specific source (i.e., "buy American," "buy union shop," "buy local"), regardless of the value offered. This may kill the incentive to be more competitive, only postponing the day of reckoning when value triumphs (as it commonly does).

Empty entitlements. Providing government services, in some cases for generations, rather than helping people to get back on their feet and provide for themselves is a sure path to dependency and helplessness.

When we encourage people to become *completely* dependent on the goodness of others for their livelihoods or achievements — when we reward people for lack of effort and personal initiative — we strip them of their confidence, trample on their dignity, and kill their will to improve themselves. Dependency purges people of their dreams, makes their spirit atrophy, and enslaves them to a lifetime of mediocrity.

We are compassionate people. We should make *every* effort to help the down-trodden get back on their feet, but we shouldn't absolve them of their personal responsibility to secure a better future for themselves and their families. As Speaker of the U.S. House of Representatives Paul Ryan once said, "We don't want to turn the safety net into a hammock that lulls able-bodied people into complacency and dependence."

Compassion shouldn't be measured by the size of a handout but by our ability to reduce dependency, enabling people to become self-sufficient and helping them to realize their dreams. Success requires powerful incentives for those who make progress — and "tough love" for those who fail to make the effort. When we offer a handout, we may satisfy someone's body and soul for an instant, but when we *invest* in people, our action may benefit them for a lifetime. Bill Clinton said it well, "We cannot build our own future without helping others to build theirs." :)

When you compete
against yourself,
you both win.

WHAT SHOULD SPORTS TEACH KIDS ABOUT LIFE?

When was the last time you attended a kid's sporting event? Whatever happened to simply enjoying an activity? Since when did we place more emphasis on "winning" than on building confidence and self-respect? Sure…some kids will translate their talent into a professional career. As for others, sports offers a wonderful learning experience about life — *if* we would just treat it that way — while "letting our kids be kids." The truth is, the lessons of sports can be applied to *all* kids' activities.

A WINNING GAME PLAN

1. Attitude is everything. Be positive. Set high expectations. Replace negative thinking with a can-do attitude.

2. Get in the game. Anyone can watch a game, but winners get off the sidelines and play. Don't let fear of failure stop you from reaching your full potential. Remember, it's better to go down swinging than to be called out on strikes.

3. Winning is as much mental as physical. Control your emotions. Stay focused and remain disciplined.

4. Master the fundamentals. Practice, practice, practice. When you master the basics, and execute them well, there's no need to worry about the score.

5. Few things come easy in life. Success is achieved through hard work and determination. It takes many years to become an overnight success.

6. Always do your best. Aim high and never settle for second best. Strive for continuous improvement in everything you do. As Coach Vince Lombardi once said, "Winning is not everything — but making the effort to win is."

7. Be ready on game day. Anyone can talk a good game. What matters is what you do when it counts.

8. Remain flexible and embrace change. You can't control the uncontrollable. So be prepared to expect the unexpected.

9. View obstacles as opportunities. When barriers get in your way, find a way around them and use them to learn and develop. Don't feel sorry for yourself.

10. Know your strengths and the strengths of others. Don't try to win games by yourself. Trust and support your teammates and they'll place their faith in you.

11. Be a team player. Be prepared to make personal sacrifices for the good of the team.

12. Keep your perspective. Competition will test your limits. Be calm, strong, and in control when it matters most.

13. Be a leader. Set high standards of excellence for yourself and others. Make people feel special and help bring out the best in everyone.

14. If you can't play fair, don't play. Integrity matters. Compete fairly and fully. When you resort to cheating, you've already lost.

15. Quitting is not an option. There will be times when things get tough. Always keep hope alive and display confidence in the eye of defeat. As Morgan Freeman said, "The best way to guarantee a loss is to quit."

16. Accept responsibility for your actions. You're in the driver's seat. Only you can decide how hard you're willing to work to achieve your goals. If you succeed, the rewards are yours. If you fail, there's always another day.

17. Learn to forgive. Forgive the mistakes of others. It may be your error that costs the team tomorrow.

18. Support others in need. Real friends are available in good times and bad. So offer your teammates encouragement and support, especially when they have a bad day.

19. Look to the future rather than the past. Don't dwell on mistakes or past defeats. Learn from the experience and move on.

20. Follow directions. Listen to your coach and respect the call of a referee, even if you disagree.

21. Compete against yourself. Competing against others may be destructive if more effort is spent tearing others down than improving your game. When you compete against yourself, however, you both win.

22. Raise your game. Find a good role model. Don't be shy to ask for help. Be open to feedback and put it to good use.

23. Say "no" to unhealthy behavior. Take care of your body. It's the only one you've got.

24. Know that losing doesn't make you a failure. Be a good loser. Bounce back after a big loss.

25. Be a good winner. Be a winner on and off the field. Be humble and quietly proud but never self-satisfied. And never let success go to your head.

HOW YOU CAN PREPARE YOUR KIDS FOR THE GAME OF LIFE

Teach your child that success doesn't come easily. Life is a continuing competition in which excellence wins. Kids aren't born with self-confidence or a positive attitude; kids don't automatically know how to conquer fear, accept feedback, overcome obstacles, or snatch victory from the jaws of defeat; kids don't always know what it's like to come back after failure, to be a humble winner, or to show grace after a terrible loss. These skills are learned. So if you aren't using every opportunity to prepare your child for the game of life, your son or daughter is being cheated out of something very special. Do your child a favor and teach him or her how to become a winner because even though it's great to win a game, it's even better to be a superstar in life. **:)**

"

Many people are
actually poor because
the only thing they have
is money.

"

8 REASONS WHY MONEY'S NOT WORTH WHAT YOU THINK

I t's easy to know how well you did in school, the soccer game, or even at work. But how do you grade success in life?

In school we receive grades; in soccer we count goals; and at work we get performance reviews. But life isn't quite that simple. We may ask ourselves: "Do I have more good days or bad days? Am I doing better today than yesterday? Am I doing better or worse than others?"

At the end of a day, we may say: "Three people smiled at me; someone thanked me for doing them a favor; and my kids told me they loved me." Not bad.

But…it's really hard to put a figure on intangibles such as a smile, a thank you, and the love of our children. And because these intangibles are difficult to quantify (and frequently not in the public eye), we often discount their true worth. Instead, we turn to more recognizable ways to measure success — *money and the things it can buy*.

If you live for money, it's time to get a life. The truth is, money can't buy everything. For example, money can't buy peace of mind, good friends, a close-knit family, work-life balance, a worry-free day, good karma, time to relax, good health, a golden anniversary, quality time with your kids, a new beginning, natural beauty, happy memories, to name just a few. Many people are actually poor because the only thing they have is money.

ARE YOU IN IT FOR THE MONEY?

Are you willing to sacrifice your dreams for more money? Some folks justify continuing in a miserable job situation by acknowledging that they're well compensated. People who live a life of purpose wake up each morning excited to pursue their dreams and make a difference. — Money can't guarantee that.

Are you willing to compromise your honor for more money? Some folks make money by being ruthless or doing unscrupulous things. People with a clear conscience have core beliefs and values that influence their decisions, shape their day-to-day actions, and determine their short- and long-term priorities. The result is that they spend more time listening to their inner voice. — Chances are, they sleep well at night.

Are you willing to squander your happiness for more money? Some people don't understand the meaning of *enough*. They think the grass is always greener on their neighbor's side of the fence. Others understand the difference between wanting and needing. As the Yiddish proverb says, "The *truly* rich are those who enjoy what they have." — Nowhere in the proverb is the word money mentioned.

Are you willing to forgo relationships for more money? Think about "the takers." You know them. They measure every action by how much they will personally benefit, while "the givers" do things without expectation of personal gain. — Which are you?

Are you willing to compromise quality of life for more money? Some people eye a prize without considering the sacrifices required to achieve it. Success has its own trade-offs. It may demand long hours, time away from family, or a significant financial commitment. The key is to understand the requirements for success before embarking on your journey. — Choose wisely.

Are you willing to forgo peace of mind for more money? There are those who feel that happiness lies in having more. As a consequence, they set very high expectations and are constantly worried and stressed out. — Do you call that happiness?

Are you willing to miss out on life for more money? Some people don't take time to smell the roses. They're so busy making money that they don't have the time to enjoy it. It's important to focus on the journey as well the destination. — There's no dress rehearsal in life.

Are you willing to cash in your personal dignity for more money? Some people are consumed with seeking the approval of others. The most important person to satisfy, however, is you. It's your life. So do your best. Be your own person. And remember, you're not finished until you do yourself proud.

I'm not saying that money isn't important, but it is important to keep money in perspective. Do you spend more money satisfying your desires than fulfilling your needs? Do you let money dictate your activities, affect your relationships, and consume your thoughts? Is money a constant cause of anxiety and a source of stress? If you answer yes to these questions, you may be becoming a slave to your money.

When you look back on your life one day, will you gauge success by the power that you attained and the wealth that you accumulated? Or will you measure the degree to which your life was rich in character and purpose? Will it matter that you led an honorable existence, made a difference in people's lives, and left the world a better place for your children? William Bruce Cameron said it well, "Not everything that can be counted counts, and not everything that counts can be counted." The choice is yours. There's more to life than money. **:)**

Most people know
how to put on a show
when a situation matters;
the key is to behave
properly even when
you think it doesn't.

MIND YOUR MANNERS

Can you read people's minds? It's not really that hard. What do people think when they see someone eat with their mouth open, slam the door in someone's face, cut someone off in the middle of a sentence, shout across the room, use foul language, look like a slob, or bark orders instead of saying "please" and "thank you"? And the list goes on. They're probably thinking "He has no manners." "She should know better." "What a loser." (Ouch.)

Manners certainly count when you're interviewing for a job, meeting your significant other's parents for the first time, or having lunch with an important customer. But manners also count even when there's no special occasion. Although friends and colleagues may not say anything, they absolutely notice, and probably judge, how you behave every day. You'd know that if you could read their minds.

WHY SHOULD YOU CARE ABOUT MANNERS?

Knowing where to place your fork and knife doesn't mean that you have good manners. Having proper manners simply means that your behavior is socially acceptable; you know how to behave so that you don't embarrass yourself, or worse yet, cause others to feel uncomfortable.

Why should you care about manners? The consequences are huge.

Show what you're made of. Good or bad manners say volumes about you and your upbringing. Manners show politeness and demonstrate an awareness of self-worth, respect for others, and a desire to fit in.

Make a good impression. You only have seconds to make a good impression. Make it positive. Remember to have a firm handshake, give your undivided attention, look him or her in the eye when you're speaking, and listen until they're finished before responding. Dress for success, but also remember your manners.

Give of yourself. Manners shift the attention from you toward others. Manners are a good way for you to show gratitude, display respect, and demonstrate kindness.

Demonstrate trustworthy behavior. Good manners are a strong indication of how you'll behave in the future. They indicate whether you're dependable, reliable, and selfless. These are critical elements in building trusting personal and business relationships. People who are rude, inconsistent, or selfish ultimately suffer the consequences.

Do yourself proud. People are judged by the company they keep. So folks may be asking themselves, "Do we want to be associated with this person?" "Would we be proud to have this person represent our organization?" "Will this individual be a good fit with our team?"

Stand out among your peers. All things being equal, good manners can set you apart from the crowd. Manners can be an important factor in achieving success.

Set an example. If you're a parent, teacher, coach, religious leader, or manager, you're influencing people every day. Make a conscious effort to be a good role model.

WHAT DO YOUR MANNERS SAY ABOUT YOU?

Some folks with poor manners offer the excuses, "I never learned" or "I don't have the time." Yet others, with huge egos, may think, "I'm the boss. Manners don't apply to me." The fact is, it doesn't take more effort to show your appreciation nor does it require more time to be pleasant. Your good manners will help make other folks feel good about themselves, as well as help others to feel good about you.

Most people know how to put on a show when a situation matters; the key is to behave properly even when you think it doesn't. The truth is, when behaviors are repeated again and again, they turn into habits. And old habits die hard. Manners matter. As Laurence Sterne, the author, said, "Respect for ourselves guides our morals; respect for others guides our manners." Don't wait for someone to remind you, or worse, don't learn from an embarrassing situation — all it requires is a conscious choice. So next time you're deciding whether to wait your turn, respond in a timely fashion, or keep someone waiting… Mind your manners! **:)**

Life is like playing
musical chairs —
you never know when
the music will stop.

HOW TO PREPARE FOR RETIREMENT

Whether we're talking about saving money, exercising, eating fruits and vegetables, or preparing for our Golden Years, the conventional wisdom is the same: A little is good, more is better. But most of us aren't doing nearly enough.

One of the things that we don't like to discuss is that we're all getting older. In fact, many of us believe that if we ignore this reality, it might go away. The problem is, failing to prepare for our Golden Years may lead to regret — never mind adding an extra burden on family members and friends. So face the facts…and cast aside the "Maybe I'll think about it tomorrow" chorus. As Napoleon Hill, the American author said, "Procrastination is the bad habit of putting off until the day after tomorrow what should have been done the day before yesterday."

GET READY FOR YOUR GOLDEN YEARS

Live before you die. Spend your time doing want-to's rather than have-to's. That's a sure way to live life without regret. As was said in the movie *Braveheart*, "Every man dies. Not every man really lives."

Be spontaneous. Don't just create a bucket list…live life hard. I know someone who waited too long and then was unable to fulfill her dreams.

Be a collector of moments, not things. Make every moment matter. As the saying goes, "Every day is an opportunity to make a new happy ending."

Reject negativity. Be positive and optimistic. Don't let regret, worry, or self-pity rob you of your precious days.

Invest your time. When you have a choice between time and money, pick time.

Pursue your dreams. Don't let fear or obstacles get in your way. Others can stop you for a moment. Only you can stop yourself for good.

Be the real you. Have the courage to live your own life rather than living the life others expect you to have. As the saying goes, "Be who you are and say what you feel because those who mind don't matter and those who matter don't mind."

Give thanks. Don't wait a lifetime to tell that special someone that you care. And if you have unresolved issues, push to gain closure.

Play show-and-tell. Prepare your friends and family to live without you. You've always been there for your friends and family. Ensure that you'll be there, in spirit, when you're gone.

Get your affairs in order. Review and update all appropriate legal documents. Make sure papers, passwords, and other key items of information are simple to find and easy to understand.

Make a difference. When most people look back on their life, they measure success by having lived life with purpose. It gives them great pleasure that they gave back more than they received.

"Wait a minute," you may be thinking. These guidelines could apply as much to a 40-year-old as to someone who's 70. The truth is, life is like playing musical chairs — you never know when the music will stop. The key is being in a position to say "I did my best" rather than "I'm not finished." So start preparing for your Golden Years. Live every day as if it were your last. One day it will be. **:)**

Shared beliefs and values form the heart of every successful relationship and ultimately determine its success.

A MARRIAGE
MADE IN HEAVEN

Remember your first date with that special someone and how it ultimately led to marriage? Upon reflection, it's abundantly clear that your entire world revolved around your partner during the courtship. Yet, as time passes, some folks take their spouse for granted. What makes a relationship last?

LET'S GET DOWN TO BASICS

Some basic elements of a successful relationship include sharing common interests, communicating on a regular basis, displaying appreciation and affection, embracing intimacy, and showing empathy. Honesty, trust, respect, and fidelity are also critical ingredients. Importantly, while the presence of these factors won't necessarily enhance the relationship, because they're expected, the absence of these qualities can turn a marriage from "heavenly" to…well, you know.

YOUR ACTIONS SPEAK FOR THEMSELVES

While best intentions are fine, daily actions form the foundation of any successful relationship. As someone once said, "Watch your thoughts, for they become words. Watch your words, for they become actions. Watch your actions, for they become habits. Watch your habits, for they become your character. And watch your character, for it becomes your destiny!" This logic also applies to successful relationships.

Here are 10 positive actions worthy of your consideration:

It's about us. Be mindful that your focus should shift from *me* to *us* and from *mine* to *ours*. That being said, it's still important to build a life together without surrendering your identity.

Be tolerant. Your spouse isn't perfect. (Neither are you.) Accept your spouse for who he or she is, rather than the person you want him or her to be.

Communicate. Practice active listening, thoughtful speaking, and constructive dialogue. Remember that silence and attention can be forms of communication, too.

Compromise, compromise, compromise. Know what's important to your spouse. Keep your spouse's needs in mind and try to be accommodating whenever possible.

Don't keep score. Be prepared to go the extra mile. Successful relationships don't have a winner and a loser. You win or lose together.

Pull your weight. A relationship doesn't require a boss. Each participant should share responsibilities based on the strengths and goals of each individual.

Manage life's ups and downs. Adversity is inevitable. The key is how you deal with it. First, acknowledge that your spouse has good intentions. Second, focus your discussions on the issue — without withdrawing, hurling insults, or getting personal. Most importantly, be supportive when the chips are down.

Keep the romance alive. Find happiness simply being in the presence of one another. As the years go by, build shared experiences and find ways to add spice to your life. Never take the relationship for granted.

Make your relationship a priority. Find balance between work and family, acknowledging that both contribute to your happiness and the strength of your relationship.

Grow older and wiser together. The most exciting part of a long-standing relationship is the growth that you achieve together.

SHARED VALUES DETERMINE SUCCESS

Shared beliefs and values form the heart of every successful relationship and ultimately determine its success. If your beliefs and values are the polar opposite of your spouse's, that can make life together difficult. The key is to understand each other's viewpoints and agree on the best way to move forward. The alternative is sweeping the issue under the rug and waiting till it rears its ugly head. Some areas where good people may differ:

Family. Do you want to have children or remain childless? Do you prefer to have a small or a large family?

Money matters. Are you a spender or a saver? How much sacrifice are you willing to make today to ensure a bright future?

Risk. How much risk are you willing to accept?

Faith. How significant is religion in your life?

Togetherness. How much time do you need alone or with "the guys" or "the girls"? How much time would you like to spend with your spouse versus with other couples?

Change. Do you prefer the familiar or do you relish change?

Roots. Are you open to moving to a different town or do you prefer remaining close to friends and family?

Decisions. Do you believe "major" decisions should be made individually or jointly?

Priorities. Do you strive for balance between home and work?

Desires. Whose needs do you place first, yours or your spouse's?

There are few things as rewarding as having a soul mate. You'll have someone who cheers you on to greatness, provides a shoulder to cry on, and helps you conquer the world. That'll make celebrations more enjoyable and setbacks more bearable. Having a soul mate will bring out the very best in you, making you the person you want to be rather than the person you are. In fact, you'll know your soul mate as well as the person in the mirror. Over time, you'll communicate with each other without even uttering a word. That'll make it seem like there's no challenge too large, no problem too insurmountable, and no dream unattainable as long as you have your soul mate by your side.

Sure, every relationship requires commitment and hard work. But it's absolutely worth it! So, never stop courting your spouse. And you'll be among the lucky couples who live happily ever after. **:)**

"

It's critical not to equate success and wealth with greed.

"

8 WAYS TO SPOT GREEDY PEOPLE

G reed is a term that describes ruthless people with naked ambition, people with an insatiable appetite for riches, those who give new meaning to the word selfish.

Greed evokes images of the rich and famous playing with lavish toys such as luxurious yachts, expensive furs, and mansions that resemble palaces. To some greedy people, it's as much about flaunting material trappings as it is about winning the game. As Gordon Gekko said in Wall Street, "It's not a question of enough, pal. It's a zero sum game, somebody wins, somebody loses."

It's critical, however, not to equate success and wealth with greed. The fact is, many successful people give generously of their wealth and/or their time. It's also true that you don't have to be particularly wealthy in order to be able to give. The fact is, greed doesn't discriminate between rich and poor. There are many ways that greed rears its ugly head every day. Here are eight ways to spot greedy people:

Life's a spectator sport. "Bystanders" who do everything they can to get out of work are greedy people. While colleagues work at a frantic pace, selfish people work hard to avoid working at all. They spend their days moving piles of papers on their desk while they watch everyone else go crazy. These folks wouldn't lift a finger if their life depended on it. When a job is complete, however, you can bet they'll be first in line to claim the rewards for the effort made (by someone else).

It's all about me. A *Christmas Carol* is an 1843 tale about Ebenezer Scrooge, a stingy and greedy businessman who has no place in his life for kindness, compassion, charity, or benevolence. In modern times, you'll find that some wealthy business executives receive an obscene year-end bonus and lavish company benefits while telling employees that the company hasn't done well enough to support annual employee raises. Why? "Because I'm worth it." But catch them in a down year, and don't be surprised when they ask others to "share the pain."

You've got my vote (as long as it doesn't affect me). Greedy people have strong opinions about issues but expect others to shoulder the burdens. These hypocrites believe that our country should go to war, as long as we send someone else's kid; the deficit should be reduced, as long as it doesn't affect their pet projects; taxes should be raised, as long as the additional taxes don't affect *their* personal pocketbook.

Something for nothing. Greedy people are first in line to ask for more but last in line to make the effort required to earn the rewards. Instead of adopting the view that everyone benefits as the pie gets larger, they view the pie as a constant — there's only so much to go around. They feel they deserve a larger piece, even at someone else's expense, and they're going to take it.

Takes all kinds. Greedy people take things that don't belong to them even at the expense of friends or colleagues. This can take the form of bluffing their way to an unwarranted promotion or accepting credit for someone else's idea. They reason that if these losers aren't smart enough to take the spoils, then the losers don't deserve them.

Gaming the system. Greedy people look for clever ways or loopholes to outsmart rules and regulations, designed to protect the system, for personal gain. Although their actions may be entirely legal, greedy people evade their responsibilities by offloading the costs to others. Examples include companies that "go right to the edge" to avoid paying taxes and politicians who waste hard-earned taxpayer money by conducting "official business" at resort destinations.

Robbing someone's confidence. Some people bring out the best in others while selfish people focus on themselves. Greedy people make themselves feel better by tearing down other people rather than by helping others feel good about themselves. Greedy people have the ability to suck the oxygen right out of a room.

Borrowing from the future. Greedy people care about their needs today and kick problems down the road. They put band-aids on problems rather than solving the root cause; they buy things that benefit their organization today rather than investing in its future; they borrow to fund their buying addiction and stick others with the bill.

We are such a competitive society. We measure success by finishing in first place, making it to the top of our game, and having better toys than our neighbors. We value instant gratification by encouraging people to consume rather than to save for a rainy day — people borrow money to prove that they live large. We idolize people who drive expensive cars, wear the latest fashions, and live in luxurious homes. Greedy or not, we all help perpetuate the addiction. When do we ever stress the importance and value of generosity over material wealth? Think about it: If enough people made a small gesture for someone else every day, we could transform the world. Do you spend more time giving or taking? **:)**

Don't wait until you desperately need a social network to begin developing one.

SIMPLIFY YOUR JOB SEARCH

Whether you're a recent college graduate or an employee looking for the Holy Grail, here are some ways to simplify your job search:

Get your mind in shape. Just as you'd want to be in peak physical shape before a big game, it's important to be in a good frame of mind before a job search. Consider beginning an exercise routine, reading a self-help book, finding an hobby that you enjoy, getting plenty of sleep, and meditating to make yourself feel better and to reduce stress. A positive attitude is key.

Ignore the law of averages. According to the Bureau of Labor Statistics, employed people work an average of 7.5 hours per day and get 8.67 hours of sleep. If these figures don't exactly apply to you, what makes you think that national unemployment averages do? So next time you hear that it's tough to find a job, remember, the unemployment rate is only a broad indicator of the job market. Even in a lousy job market, people get job offers every day. It may as well be you.

Don't fool yourself. Some people think, "My phone will start ringing when I begin my job search." Yeah, sure. When was the last time someone called you with a job opportunity? Dreams, unlike eggs, don't hatch from sitting on them.

Cash isn't the only currency. Some people forgo opportunities if they don't provide big bucks. The fact is, every experience that you gain is an investment in your future. If you leave your job, you'll take that experience with you and cash it in for a bigger prize.

If the shoe fits. Put yourself in the employer's shoes. Would you rather hire someone referred by a person you trust or meet someone unknown? So, network, network, network.

Are you playing bumper cars? Unfortunately, some people treat networking like a game of bumper cars in which progress is measured by the number of people they run into rather than the quality of the underlying relationships. Simply put, just handing out more business cards and adding more friends to Facebook or LinkedIn isn't networking. Don't wait until you desperately need a social network to begin developing one. Networks are built on trust, respect, and personal chemistry — that doesn't happen overnight.

Roll with the punches. Don't be bullheaded. If Plan "A" doesn't go exactly as expected, be prepared to roll with the punches. You may have to modify your expectations. Your new job may require a longer commute, lower salary, or accepting a different type of job than the one you had your sights on. This is your Plan "B." It doesn't mean you should settle for the first opportunity that comes along or, worse, sell your soul. It does mean you may have to compromise. Remember, broadening your search doesn't mean you have to accept any job that is offered, but you should give serious consideration to any offer you receive. Maybe Plan "B" will work out better after all.

Are you swimming against the tide? Rip currents are powerful channel currents of water flowing away from the shore. Many people swept out to sea try to fight their way back by swimming against the current. That's how people drown, from exhaustion. The fact is, people who remain calm and swim parallel to the shore swim out of the current and to safety. The same is true with a job search. Remember to go with the flow.

How do you measure success? Some people beat themselves up if they don't get a job in a week. Like the legendary football coach Vince Lombardi, I believe you don't have to worry about winning games if you focus on fundamentals such as blocking and tackling. So don't concentrate on getting the job; instead, focus on the quality activity that you generate. Every good interview or meeting with a member of your network brings you one step closer to your goal.

It takes two to tango. Some applicants feel that potential employers hold all the cards during the hiring process. The fact is, organizations need great talent as much as you want a great employer. Be selective. It'll be a win-win proposition.

If you believe you can't, you won't. A job search doesn't have to be a terrible experience. It's the beginning of an exciting new opportunity. Have fun. Reconnect with members of your network. And remember your experience so that you can lend a helpful hand to someone in need once you've landed your great new job.

I would say good luck, but you won't need it. You'll be making your own. **:)**

If you don't know
why you'd hire you,
neither will they.

HOW TO ACE
YOUR JOB
INTERVIEW

Be selective. An employer can tell if you're serious about a job interview or going through the motions. ∎ The key is to be selective enough that you're willing to make the investment. If you're not excited about the opportunity, odds are they won't be excited about you.

2. Do your homework. An interview starts long before the actual meeting takes place.

- Do you know anyone who works for the employer — even if they work in a different area than the one you're applying to?

- What can they tell you about the company? Can they provide you with an introduction or say something on your behalf?

- Who will be conducting the interview? What's his or her background?

- What do you know about the company? Did you visit their website and read the annual report? Do they discuss key initiatives, company values, and their culture? Has the company been in the news lately? What do analysts say about their strengths and weaknesses? What does their recruiting information say about the people who work there?

3. Put yourself in their shoes. If you were conducting the interview, what qualities and skills would you be looking for? What things might disqualify a candidate?

4. Practice, practice, practice. What makes you a good fit for the organization? What will excite the interviewer or pose potential problems for you? Try to anticipate questions and prepare responses. Run your answers past a friend. The key is to think through your answers *before* the interview.

Some of the most common questions may include: Why do you want to work for this company? Why should we hire you? What do you like most and least about your current job? What are your strengths and weaknesses? Remember, real-life stories and hard facts will bring your responses to life.

You'll also be asked if you have any questions of the employer. Some questions worth consideration include: What are you looking for in an ideal candidate? What are the opportunities for growth?

5. You're always onstage. Some people believe that an applicant is evaluated based solely on the interview. The truth is, you will be judged on everything that takes place before, during, and after the interview. How will that Facebook post go over when the potential employer catches a glimpse? Employers will also note whether your résumé was sent with a customized cover letter; whether you were responsive in answering phone calls and e-mails; whether you were courteous to the person confirming the interview; and whether you followed up in a timely manner.

6. Be focused. What key points do you want to make during your interview? Are you sure they address key factors in the employer's selection criteria?

7. Differentiate yourself. What qualifications or experiences make you uniquely qualified for the position? What can you do or say that'll differentiate you from other applicants?

8. Be yourself. Enjoy yourself during the interview. If you're comfortable, you'll make the interviewer feel at ease. Think through your answers before the interview takes place. But remember, if you try to fake your way through the interview, believe me, it will show!

9. Remain confident. Confidence comes with practice. Did you research the company? Did you identify questions and prepare responses? Did you select key points that you want to drive home? Most of all, remember: If you don't know why you'd hire you, neither will they.

10. Stand out. What can you do to stand out from the crowd? Do you have any personal interests that'll make you memorable?

11. No-no's. There are several things that will knock you out of the running. Here are a few: Spell-check all correspondence. Then READ through everything again to catch those "misused" words that spell-check overlooked. Make sure that you dress properly and are appropriately groomed. When in doubt, it's better to be overdressed than too casual. Show up for the interview 5 or 10 minutes early. Make sure you can answer basic questions, such as why you want the job or why you chose their company. If there are time gaps or other issues in your résumé be prepared to address them. Don't use foul language or bad-mouth your previous employer. Don't bring up controversial subjects such as politics or religion, and don't disclose confidential information about your company. Last, don't try to do an end run around someone during the application process. (Ouch.)

12. Don't put all your eggs in one basket. Some people fall in love with one job opportunity and stop all other activity. The truth is, even if the opportunity looks like a shoo-in, it could dry up for no apparent reason.

13. Look in the mirror. After every interview, ask yourself what you'd do differently if you had the opportunity to go through the interview again.

14. May the "luck" be with you. Sometimes you can do everything perfectly, but the job is offered to someone else. When this happens, don't spend time beating yourself up. Move forward. The interview process takes determination, persistence, and a touch of luck. If you follow these tips, you'll be one step ahead of the others, so luck won't be required. But good luck anyway! **:)**

"

Keeping score,
in friendships,
is a losing game.

"

GOOD FRIENDS DON'T KEEP SCORE

Keeping score may be appropriate in sports, but it doesn't do much to foster a meaningful relationship. In fact, it doesn't matter whether it's a relationship between friends, married couples, or work colleagues…keeping score is highly destructive. Yet some folks are so obsessed with keeping the scales equally balanced that they're one step away from creating a spreadsheet.

"I washed the dishes so you take out the garbage." "I paid for the gas so you pick up the tip." "I stayed late last time, the least you can do is…"

Who's up? Who's down? Who cares?

WHAT HAVE YOU DONE FOR ME LATELY?

Any way you cut it, keeping score is damaging. Here are some of the costs:

Unproductive. What are you trying to prove? Are you trying to win brownie points for doing something kind, or trying to ensure that you don't get the raw end of the deal? In any case, when a relationship turns competitive, someone is made to feel uncomfortable.

Dissatisfying. Keeping score creates an uncomfortable feeling of obligation. It's no longer unconditional giving; it's giving with strings attached. It shifts the emphasis from *"want to"* to *"have to."*

Destructive. Keeping score changes the focus from *us* to *me*. A me-centered friendship can lead to bitterness and resentment — poisoning the relationship over time.

Small-minded. Keeping score fosters a feeling of "what have you done for me lately?" at the expense of investing in a long-term relationship. Keeping score turns a friendship into a competition.

Come to think of it — what *are* the rules of this game? Is taking the kids to school worth more or less than helping the kids with their homework? Is bringing home a larger paycheck valued more or less than providing emotional support during tough times? If you do something for me today, how much time do I have to even the score? If you pay for something, do I have to buy something of equal value even though you make more money? Is making dinner worth more or less than taking you out? If this sounds absurd, that's because it is!

KEEPING SCORE, IN FRIENDSHIPS, IS A LOSING GAME

Together we're a team. Healthy friendships are a team effort in which everyone wins or loses together. Emphasis should be placed on attaining your mutual goals rather than on scoring points.

In you I trust. Trust stems, in part, from knowing that someone has your back. Keeping score breeds mistrust and unnecessary anxiety. Time can be better spent doing something meaningful.

Focus on the big picture. If friendships are forever, why is so much emphasis placed on short-term gain? Like anything else of value, relationships require an investment.

Keep game-playing on the field. The desire to measure everything is a colossal waste of time. Instead, do what's right and the rest should take care of itself.

LIFE IS BETTER WHEN YOU DON'T KEEP SCORE

How do you keep score when people use different scoring systems? Should a deed be measured by its monetary value or by the effort made? Do three small acts equal one big one? Is a monetary contribution worth more than an emotional one? What happens if a gesture is so momentous that it can't be returned? To make matters more difficult, people often inflate their own contribution and minimize their partner's actions. For these reasons, and more, keeping score doesn't add up.

In any good relationship, people give willingly of themselves without an expectation of getting something in return. The reward is not personal gain but rather, making the other person happy. Of course, you will have periods when you take on more responsibility, and your spouse, friend, or colleague will do the same, but over the course of a lifetime, things even out. Will it come out evenly? Probably not, but that's the point. The joy is in the giving.

In healthy relationships, there's no game-playing. You place the interests of your spouse, friend, or colleague ahead of your own, and they do the same for you — no questions asked. This isn't determined by formal agreement. The commitment is much stronger. It's called a relationship, and it's where you share, grow, and benefit *together*. There's no need to second-guess the intentions of your partner in this relationship or for your partner to doubt yours. You both know that the real reward is the relationship — the bonus is what you build together. As someone said, "A friend is someone who does things that count, but doesn't stop to count them." So save the scorekeeping for the field. Play ball. **:)**

Forgiving doesn't mean forgetting, nor does it mean approving of, what someone did. It just means that you're letting go of the anger toward that person.

THE POWER TO FORGIVE

We've all experienced some level of hurt and disappointment in our lives. It may have taken the form of a friend who betrayed us, a family member who disappointed us, a superior who exploited us, or an individual who caused some harm to our loved one. While some wounds are shallow and relatively easy to dismiss, others run deep, causing some to harbor anger or seek revenge. Others choose a second option…to forgive and forget.

Seeking retaliation, rather than forgiveness, traps you in the anger. In fact, some people become so consumed by their bitterness that it harms them physically and mentally. The truth is, studies have found that forgiving is good for the body and the soul. As Buddha taught, "Holding on to anger is like grasping a hot coal with the intent of throwing it at someone else; you are the one who gets burned."

WHY IS FORGIVENESS SO HARD TO SWALLOW?

No one said that forgiving is easy. Here are some reasons why:

Revenge makes us feel better. The only way offenders can really know the hurt they inflicted is to experience it themselves. So we seek an eye for an eye.

Revenge will prohibit a repeat offense. While we can't undo what's already happened, we want to ensure that it isn't repeated. So we mount an aggressive campaign against the responsible party.

We desire justice. We're cynical that justice will be served. Therefore, the only way to "even the score" is through revenge.

We see no sign of remorse. We want closure. The problem is, the offender shows no sign of regret for the pain that he or she caused.

There's little chance of rehabilitation. We reason that some people are just bad apples with little prospect for change. We're concerned that they'll receive leniency and repeat the offense.

It's difficult to let go of the anger. Some people cause so much anguish that we find it inconceivable to forgive them for the grief they caused.

The key is that forgiving doesn't mean forgetting, nor does it mean approving of, what someone did. It just means that you're letting go of the anger toward that person.

THE POWER OF FORGIVENESS

There are several benefits to forgiveness. From a moral imperative, turning your cheek is the right thing to do. Period. Furthermore, it's a lot healthier and takes a lot less energy to forgive someone than to hold a grudge and remain angry. The fact is, when you're consumed by bitterness, resentment, and vengeance, you can get swallowed up by your anger. As Lewis B. Smedes, the renowned theologian, said, "To forgive is to set a prisoner free and discover that the prisoner was you."

Forgiveness does not mean suppressing your feelings or pretending the anger doesn't exist. Instead, forgiveness requires a conscious decision to release your resentment and thoughts of revenge. It also calls on you to acknowledge and practice the full range of emotions that you possess, such as grief and anger as well as kindness and compassion — even toward someone who has hurt you deeply.

That's tough, you say? It's important to remind yourself that one of the main reasons to show forgiveness is to benefit yourself. Hate is a cancer on one's soul. It can cause you to feel helpless and frustrated and trap you in a never-ending cycle of anger and resentment. And although you may have every reason to be bitter, you will be compounding the problem by keeping the issue alive. Think of it this way: While they hurt you once, now you're doing it to yourself.

The truth is, forgiveness reduces the offender's grip on you and helps you focus on other, positive areas of your life. So follow the wisdom of Robert Brault, the author, who said, "If you can't forgive and forget, pick one." **:)**

People stop trying when there's no benefit for being exceptional and no consequence for being mediocre.

DO YOU PROMOTE EXCELLENCE?

Every organization needs the best and brightest people to join its team. It needs trailblazers who hit the ball out of the park and light a path for others to follow. Why in the world would anyone penalize these shining stars for their excellence? But the sad fact is that we do it every day.

Think of the salesperson who breaks a sales record. Instead of recognizing him for a job well done, we cap his earnings because we're afraid he makes too much money. (Does that make sense?) Think of the young teacher who's so good at what she does that her kids don't want to go home at the end of the day. Instead of promoting her as a role model, we resent her for making the other teachers look bad. (Is that fair?) Or think of the entrepreneur who goes from nothing to the pinnacle of success. Instead of celebrating her as proof of the American Dream, we bad-mouth her for being successful. (Give me a break!)

Why do we demand excellence and then penalize people for achieving it? Don't we see that we're turning them off? Don't we understand that we're discouraging others from following their lead? Don't we realize that we're promoting mediocrity when we lower the bar, again and again, just so we don't offend anyone? It makes no sense! The fact is, when you discourage excellence, you get less of it. Period!

If you want excellence, you can't give the mediocre student the same grade as the terrific one; you can't grant the mediocre employee the same reward as the superstar; and you can't award the team that finishes last the same prize as the one that finishes first. "Why not," you say? When you fail to recognize and/or reward exceptional performance, you raise the obvious question, "Why should I care if they don't?"

Next time you look around an organization and experience a sea of mediocrity, where no one cares, ask yourself, "Is apathy their fault or the organization's failing?" When people say, "I can't" or "I won't," it produces the same results. People stop trying when there's no benefit for being exceptional and no consequence for being mediocre.

EXCEPTIONAL PERFORMANCE BEGINS WITH YOU

You should want the salesperson to break the bank because if his sales are off the charts, your company is benefiting, too; you should want the teacher to go above and beyond because if others follow her lead, all of our kids benefit; you should want every entrepreneur to be a raging success because it provides hope for everyone else — "If she did it, I can too."

It's time to raise the bar. It's time to bring out the best in people. It's time to demand excellence, and to recognize and reward it, too. We don't gain anything from lowering the bar so that everyone can clear it. We also don't gain anything by denying people the rewards they richly deserve. If we really want exceptional performance, we have no choice but to treat exceptional people in an exceptional way. **:)**

If your entire business were dependent on one customer, would you treat that one customer better than all your other customers?

THANKS FOR A JOB WELL DONE

Why are we surprised when a salesperson knows her stuff? A contractor honors his promises? Or a company lives up to its claims? Isn't that the way it should be? It's unfortunate that we get excited when someone does his or her job properly.

Think about it. Are we asking too much for an airplane to leave on time, a restaurant to be clean, or a company's product literature to tell us the *whole* story? I don't think so. How about a receptionist who doesn't have attitude, a merchant who returns calls promptly, or a website that doesn't contain typos? You get the point.

Of course, apathetic people, who simply don't care, cause some of these issues. Other times, it's due to management that tolerates mediocrity — an organization that lowers the bar so low you can trip over it. The result, however, is still the same...they're going nowhere fast. The fact is, it's not enough just to come to work, it's about getting the job done right.

JOB #1: CREATE A CULTURE OF EXCELLENCE

Since superior client service is as much a philosophy as an activity, it's important to discover just what kind of culture produces the mind-set necessary to exceed customer expectations. Ask yourself, do we:

- Strive for excellence or settle for mediocrity?
- Treat customers differently *now* than when we were courting them?
- Focus on getting things right or consider inaccuracies to be a way of life?
- Build long-term relationships or promote short-term sales?
- Make policy changes to benefit customers or for employee convenience?
- Spend our time adding customer value or filling out internal paperwork?
- Anticipate customer needs or scramble when relationships are in jeopardy?
- Make ourselves accessible when customers need us or only when it's convenient for us?
- Discipline unethical behavior or turn our back on disgraceful conduct?
- Promote employee continuity or look like a turnstile?
- Spend time in front of customers or in staff meetings?
- Provide exceptional value or compensate for inadequacies by trying to be friendly?
- Solicit customer feedback or think that we know it all?
- Promote clear and transparent communication or use confusing technical jargon?

- Benchmark against the best in class or sweep our inadequacies under the rug?

- Protect customer privacy *before* or *after* issues arise?

- Challenge the status quo or rest on our laurels?

- Stimulate trust by being dependable or lose faith by being unpredictable?

- Address customer issues promptly or respond when time permits?

- Build trust by following through on promises made or by "talking a good game"?

- Value trust as much as we cherish profitability?

IT COMES WITH THE JOB

If your entire business were dependent on one customer, would you treat that *one* customer better than *all* your other customers? If so, ask yourself why. Shouldn't every customer be special? Sure…it's not possible to give every customer your undivided attention. But it's more than reasonable to meet or exceed their expectations every day. If that's not happening, shame on you. Excellence should be the rule, not the exception.

Doing a great job is as much an attitude as it is an activity. As Jonas Salk, the medical doctor and researcher, said, "The reward for work well done is the opportunity to do more." So give it your best. Excellence is not a destination, but a way of life. Every time you hear "Thanks for doing a good job," you'll know you're on the right course. **:)**

Feedback is helpful and constructive; criticism is hurtful and damaging.

CRITICISM IS NOT FEEDBACK

Feedback is a vital element of our personal and professional development. But in order for input to have tangible benefits, two principles must be followed. First, it must be supportive. The fact is, there's a huge difference between feedback and criticism. Feedback is helpful and constructive; criticism is hurtful and damaging. Second, input alone won't amount to anything if the recipient doesn't modify their behavior accordingly. Listed below are tips to make feedback a more effective and rewarding experience for both giver and recipient.

18 WAYS TO *GIVE* BETTER FEEDBACK

SETTING THE STAGE

Make your input count. Give feedback that is *factual* — based on hard evidence — rather than emotional; is *even-handed* — examines both sides of an issue; is *balanced* — sees the positive and the negative; and is *open-minded* — free from personal bias.

Make the feedback timely. Offer input soon after an activity rather than weeks or months later. This will ensure that the feedback is relevant and helpful.

Give feedback in person. Input doesn't have to be formal, but it should be made a priority. For that reason, it's important to give feedback face-to-face, or via "Skype" if necessary, rather than by e-mail or text. This will enhance communication by providing a more personal and immediate two-way dialog and will enable each party to gauge the other's body language.

Give feedback *prior* thought. Know the key points that you want to make rather than shooting from the hip.

Provide advance notification. Don't blindside the recipient by catching them off guard. Furthermore, ease into the conversation rather than hitting them with a two-by-four.

Respect the recipient's other priorities. Catch the recipient during a peaceful time of day so that they're emotionally available. Remember, being present is not the same as being there.

Refrain from multitasking. Before providing feedback, secure the recipient's undivided attention — free from distractions.

THE FEEDBACK

Build people up rather than tearing them down. Compliment people in public; present their shortcomings in private. Avoid shaming or threatening the recipient at all costs.

Focus on the act. Base your input on the recipient's actions rather than on demeaning the person.

Be constructive. Make your feedback *actionable* rather than general.

Be honest and direct. Tell it like it is. This will ensure that nothing is left to the imagination. Furthermore, if your feedback is always glowing, compliments will be less credible.

Praise, the right way. A compliment is great — when it offers *specifics* about what the person is doing right or areas where they've improved.

Present the facts. Feedback should always come from firsthand experience rather than something you heard via a third party.

Encourage meaningful communication. Make feedback a two-way conversation rather than a *lecture*. Furthermore, the reviewer and recipient must *communicate* with each other rather than just taking turns talking. And — please give the recipient ample time to respond.

Be conscious of what goes unsaid. Read between the lines. A recipient who is silent could still be sending you a loud message.

AFTER THE FACT

Confirm understanding. Make sure you and the recipient are on the same page before ending the conversation.

Establish an action plan. Offer suggestions for improvement and expectations going forward.

Follow up. Establish a specific time to review actions taken and progress being made.

ARE YOU OPEN TO FEEDBACK?

Some people avoid feedback like the plague. They think that if they don't know their flaws, they don't have any. It shouldn't come as a surprise that these folks make the same mistakes over and over again. Other people evade constructive feedback by surrounding themselves with yes people. They'd rather receive confirmation of their own ideas than be challenged by opposing views. While that might do wonders for their ego, it does little to advance their cause. The fact is, surrounding yourself with yes people is like talking to yourself.

Feedback should be welcomed rather than feared. In fact, we should thank folks who make the effort to nurture us with their valuable input — even if it hurts at times. How do you expect to become a better person if you don't know where to begin? The truth is, practice doesn't make perfect if you're doing it wrong. Feedback enables us to learn about our shortcomings and take corrective action. Don't bury your head…nourish it. That's how excellence is born. **:)**

"

Being a good loser helps build character, provides valuable lessons, and helps you become mentally prepared for your next challenge.

"

HOW TO LOSE AND STILL COME OUT A WINNER

It's easy to be a good winner, but do you have what it takes to be a good loser? It's hard to lose when you've worked tirelessly to achieve a goal, when friends and family come out to support you — and you don't want to let them down. Of course, any loss can be heartbreaking, and even embarrassing, given that everyone knows the score and there's nowhere to hide. But even though losing can be unnerving, being a good loser is essential to becoming a winner.

Being a good loser does not mean being content with failing or condoning a half-baked effort. Instead, being a good loser helps build character, provides valuable lessons, and helps you become mentally prepared for your next challenge.

THIS IS HOW LOSERS LOSE

Whether failure becomes a stepping-stone or a stumbling block depends on how you handle it. Here are six ways poor losers react to a situation:

Wallow in self-pity. Some people feel so sorry for themselves that it becomes all-consuming. They drag themselves down.

Shut down. Some folks refuse to talk to anyone and shut themselves off from the rest of the world.

Deflect personal responsibility. Some people spend time and effort creating excuses, pointing fingers, and casting blame for their loss.

Develop a victim mindset. Some folks think the world is unfair and feel they've been mistreated. This can lead to destructive negative emotions such as anger, envy, and even hatred.

Acquire a self-defeatist attitude. Some people beat themselves up, believing that one loss makes them a failure. This can develop into a chronic pessimism in which they refuse to get back on the horse.

Remain stuck in the past. Some folks harbor on a defeat rather than look forward to their next opportunity.

WINNERS KNOW HOW TO LOSE

Your ability to maintain a positive attitude, learn, and move forward will determine whether you win or lose in the future. Here are eight guidelines to consider:

Take time to mourn the loss. It's natural to get upset after a loss. Give it a good cry and move on.

Be positive. Winning without honor is worse than a loss. Hold your head up high. Remain calm and level-headed. Tomorrow's another day.

Remain true to your values. These are the times when real leaders reveal their character. Show some grace and self-control. Be a positive role model. Do yourself proud.

Own the loss. Don't look for excuses or cast blame. Accept responsibility for the loss or you'll never take corrective action to better yourself.

Determine why you lost. If the loss was due to poor effort or careless errors, shame on you. It's one thing to lose to a better opponent and quite another to beat yourself.

Raise your game. What can you do differently next time you're faced with a similar situation? Learn and improve.

Turn barriers into hurdles. Don't let challenges deter you from your goal. Winners run toward challenges; losers run from them.

Don't quit. Show some grit and determination. One loss doesn't make you a loser any more than one win makes you a winner. As Norman Cousins, the political journalist, said, "Death is not the greatest loss in life. The greatest loss is what dies inside us while we live."

YOU WIN SOME, YOU LOSE SOME

Some people believe there shouldn't be losers — every participant should be a winner. I believe losing is an important part of life. Losing makes you self-reliant; it's an opportunity to accept responsibility for your own destiny. Losing builds confidence and makes you strong; it inspires you to weather setbacks in the future. Losing teaches you humility; it keeps you grounded. Losing provides valuable lessons; it proves that no matter how good you are, you can always become better. Losing fosters determination; it proves that when you're steadfast, you can overcome almost any challenge in life. Last, but not least, losing builds character. As Chilon of Sparta, one of the "Seven Sages of Greece," said, "Prefer a loss to a dishonest gain; the one brings pain at the moment, the other for all time." The bottom line is that you can lose and still come out a winner. Think about it…what do you stand to lose? **:)**

The best networkers
have learned that,
as with anything in life,
what goes around,
comes around.

THE GIVE AND TAKE OF NETWORKING

L ooking for a job? Need some personal advice? Looking to make some valuable connections? Perhaps you should try networking, but only consider it if you're prepared to help others first. Otherwise, your efforts will fall short.

Unfortunately, some people treat networking like a game of bumper cars in which progress is measured by the number of people that they run into rather than the quality of the underlying relationships created. Simply put, just adding more friends to Facebook or LinkedIn is "notworking."

Others treat networking like a personal marketing campaign dedicated to spreading the word about themselves and their needs, while ignoring the needs of their peers. This "me-first thinking" not only won't work, but it's actually counterproductive. Still other folks reach out to others only when they need something. And then they're surprised when their requests produce little.

HOW TO MAKE NETWORKING WORK

To be part of a successful network, it's important to follow a few basic rules.

1. Don't wait until you desperately need a network to begin developing one. Networks are based on trust, respect, and personal chemistry — that doesn't happen overnight.

2. Join a social network or an industry or professional association to add structure to your professional relationships while expanding your network.

3. Know your personal strengths and the strengths of each member of your network. This information will come in handy in helping others.

4. If you join a group get involved rather than sitting on the sidelines.

5. Group get-togethers are not substitutes for one-on-one meetings. Large gatherings tend to have "fixed agendas," making it difficult for members to open up personally. Furthermore, a few members may dominate discussions.

6. Keep in touch with members of your network on a regular basis or you'll drift apart.

NETWORKING ETIQUETTE

Successful networking occurs when people come together based on mutual respect and common interests, and then voluntarily provide support for others with no strings attached. They believe that by helping others, they'll eventually help themselves. Here are a few guidelines:

- Make the first move in the relationship. Be a giver not a taker.

- Only make promises that you can keep. Managing expectations is key.

- Like gift giving, give people what they want, not what you want them to have.

- If you *can't* fulfill a request, recommend someone who can.

- Evaluate the reasonableness of your requests.

- Know what you want before making a request.

- Be specific. If you're vague, you may end up getting something that you don't need or want.

- Respect people's priorities. They may have a lot on their plate. Be understanding if they can't help you right away.

- When a friend introduces you to a colleague, make him or her "look good." Furthermore, keep your friend in the loop.

- Never take someone's good nature for granted; a thank-you is always required.

- Don't keep score. Just because you performed a favor doesn't guarantee one in return.

- When you do someone a favor, don't make a big deal out of it. Do it to help, or don't do it at all.

- Don't push yourself on people. They'll ask for assistance if they need it.

- Don't show off by proving how much you know when a quick answer will suffice.

- Make sure you're contacting people at a convenient time.

- Don't become too reliant on any one individual.

- Don't ask for sensitive information; be aware of the costs of your request — in both time and money; and make sure your requests are ethical and reasonable.

- When someone trusts you with sensitive information, maintain its privacy.

- Don't judge other people's requests.

Those who are successful at networking will tell you that its potential is unlimited. It only stands to reason that the people who benefit most are the "givers" — those who go all-out to help others — rather than the "takers" — those who are merely out for personal gain. The best networkers have learned that, as with anything in life, what goes around, comes around. **:)**

"

We've become
so addicted to instant
gratification that we're
blind to the impact it
has on our lives.

"

ARE YOU SELLING YOUR FUTURE SHORT?

Today we're all about living in the moment. Who knows what tomorrow will bring, right? We respond by seeking instant gratification. For example, it's easier to watch TV than to exercise; it's more fun to go out with friends than to study for the exam; and it's more exciting to buy a new "toy" than to save for a rainy day.

The problem is, we've become so accustomed to instant gratification that we've lost sight of the consequences that it has on our future. In other words, we believe we can live "high on the hog" today and hope that tomorrow will take care of itself. Well, it doesn't always work that way. Our short-term wants and desires often work contrary to our long-term interests. As Neal A. Maxwell, the author and educator, said, "Never give up what you want most for what you want today."

WHAT'S THE IMPACT OF INSTANT GRATIFICATION?

Winning at any cost. Some folks act like bulldozers to get ahead. They don't care if they win by trampling people or by selling their soul to the devil. To them, it's not how you play the game, but winning that counts.

If you care about integrity: Tomorrow matters. People with a long-term outlook value honesty and integrity. They know the difference between right and wrong and let their conscience be their guide as they pursue their dreams. Their reputation speaks for itself.

Putting personal needs ahead of others. Takers are like sharks, trolling the waters, with appetites that are never satisfied. Their selfishness knows no bounds.

If you care about relationships: Tomorrow matters. People with a long-term outlook value relationships. They recognize the importance of generosity and doing right by others, even if it means sacrificing their own interests. Givers use every opportunity to create lasting, win-win relationships.

Living "high on the hog" rather than within one's means. Some folks spend more than they earn. College bills? Unforeseen expenses? Retirement? They'll figure that out tomorrow — often when they can least afford it.

If you care about your finances: Tomorrow matters. People with a long-term perspective live within their means. They know that some expenses are inevitable and they begin saving early — while their savings compound over time. This is in contrast to people who pay finance charges each month and never have anything to show for it.

Desiring quick-fix remedies over personal sacrifice. Some people desire good health as long as it doesn't require them to abandon bad habits. Instead, they resort to quick-fix remedies that require minimal personal sacrifice.

If you care about your health: Tomorrow matters. People who care about their long-term well-being embrace a healthy lifestyle. They make healthy food choices, maintain a steady exercise routine, and take steps to enhance their mental and emotional health. These habits are supported by a dose of personal discipline that reveals true character and common sense.

Opting to keep the peace rather than disciplining children. Some folks are absentee parents even when they're actually present. They allow their kids to run wild, and they surrender authority at the first sign of a tantrum, choosing not to make a scene. Of course, they expect others to discipline *their* kids and teach *them* proper values and respect.

> *If you care about quality parenting: Tomorrow matters.* Behind every good kid are parents or caregivers who understand the importance of raising them that way. These adults are passionate about offering a quality education, instilling good values, providing discipline, and serving as exemplary role models.

BLINDED BY INSTANT GRATIFICATION

We've become so addicted to instant gratification that we're blind to the impact it has on our lives — we're simply trading away our future potential for happiness today. The truth is, instant gratification makes our lives more complicated and less fulfilling. It adds to the uncertainty and volatility that we experience every day. So why add to life's unpredictability by making choices that ultimately lead to stress and anxiety?

There's no need to starve today by focusing entirely on tomorrow. By combining a little sacrifice, patience, and discipline, the future can be bright. The alternative is to be tempted by the "forbidden fruit" of instant gratification and be forced to accept the rotten consequences. **:)**

Taking a calculated risk is not the same as gambling. One is taking a risk after considered judgment; the other is leaving everything to the roll of the dice.

WINGING IT THROUGH LIFE

All too often, people who wing it, and succeed, are greeted with admiration. Their success is viewed as a magical ability to ignore hard work, hope for the best, and still come out on top. To them, winging it is a way of life.

Winging it is a form of shooting craps. You gamble that, prepared or not, you'll be able to handle whatever comes up in life — sevens or snake eyes. But even veteran gamblers recognize that the odds are stacked against them. Taking a calculated risk is not the same as gambling. One is taking a risk after considered judgment; the other is leaving everything to the roll of the dice.

Originally, the term "winging it" was used to describe actors who relied on prompters in the wings because they never took the time to learn their lines. Winging it, or bluffing, certainly didn't enhance the reputation of the actor who was performing without adequate preparation. And it won't help you.

WINGING IT IS NOTHING MORE THAN A GAMBLE

You may have confidence in your ability to make off-the-cuff decisions; indeed, winging it may even be a habit, one you have little desire to break because it hasn't created a major problem for you — yet.

The fact is, it's impossible to substitute winging it for planning, preparation, and practice. When people wing it, they hope everything will work out, but they don't know that it will. As a result of laziness or a tendency to operate on automatic pilot, they forget that making things work takes work. As Jascha Heifetz, the renowned violinist, said, "If I don't practice one day, I know it; two days, the critics know it; three days, the public knows it."

Practicing the basics, being prepared, and following up on details is a small price to pay for success. Crisis management — putting out fires all day long — is more expensive and it's exhausting. Winging it wastes valuable time and energy, leads to a loss of credibility, and can damage even the most promising career.

Of course, there will always be unpleasant surprises to deal with because the world isn't perfect. But you can reduce the number of crises that plague you (and the stress they cause) by maintaining discipline in areas that are controllable.

How do you stop this runaway freight train and gain control of your life? The answer is as simple as an old Chinese proverb: "A journey of a thousand miles begins with a single step."

Since winging it has much in common with gambling, the first step is to follow the precept that Gamblers Anonymous requires of new members: Admit that you're a gambler. Once you see yourself as a gambler (rather than an astute, risk-taking person), you've taken that first important step. When you've convinced yourself that you must break out of your winging-it, shoot-from-the-hip, flip-a-coin mentality, you'll have a new lease on life. Once you incorporate some planning and preparation into your life, I'm sure you'll find that the investment leads to better, more reliable outcomes. Is it worth the effort? You bet! **:)**

Engaging in risky behavior is no different from gambling.

LIVING LIFE
ON THE EDGE!

S ome people live life on the edge and love every minute of it. They get a rush from taking on seemingly insurmountable challenges and beating the odds, while others roll the dice with their finances, pursuing an insatiable, shark-like hunger for material wealth.

Engaging in risky behavior is no different from gambling. Whether you bet the ranch on a get-rich-quick scheme, buy too much stuff on credit, or ignore your doctor's warnings — the result is the same — a willingness to risk it all.

WHAT DO YOU HAVE TO LOSE?

Let's look at six bets that are placed every day:

Getting rich quick. There'll always be get-rich-quick schemes and the people to fund them. Whether it's the next gold rush, dot-com investing, or flipping homes, these folks try their luck in the hope of "winning the lottery." Unfortunately, most of these schemes end the same way…disappointment, indebtedness, or worse. Like musical chairs, if you can't find a chair when the music stops, you're out of the game. In the game of life, you're also out of luck.

Living large. Some people, like sharks, spend their entire life hunting and consuming. All the oceans in the world can't satisfy these eating machines. When the sharks can't afford their buying addiction, they purchase their "toys" on credit. The problem is, if they're not careful, they'll be making hefty monthly finance payments without receiving anything tangible in return. Whatever happened to living within your means, much less saving money for a rainy day?

Betting the ranch. Whoa, partner! If you don't guard your personal wealth against downside risk, you're leaving yourself vulnerable to substantial loss and may not even know it. Just think about those entrepreneurs who fail to protect their businesses by not incorporating. They may wind up sacrificing all their personal assets if they get sued and lose in court. A similar example comes from one of the biggest causes of personal bankruptcy: the onset of serious illness without adequate health insurance coverage. And if that happens, there goes the ranch — and that's no bull.

Taking care of business. How many times do people receive advice to drop five pounds, stop smoking, exercise 30 minutes each day, or lay off the fried foods? Sometimes this advice is a preventive measure. Other times, it's given to someone rehabilitating from an illness. Don't wait till it's too late to heed the warning. Take care of business (it's your life) and be around to enjoy the payoff.

Facing the facts. Some events are so remote that their chance of happening is as likely as sighting a black swan. The truth is, some people also adopt this philosophy in life. Why purchase disability insurance? Who needs a will? Chances are it'll never happen — until it does. Some eternal optimists fail to anticipate downside risks or the need to save for a rainy day. Then, if something unexpected occurs, it creates havoc in their life. That's why they make umbrellas.

Putting all your eggs in one basket. If you place all your eggs in one basket, any fall will be a messy one. This truism applies in cases where one client represents too large a percentage of your company's sales; where most of your money is concentrated in a handful of investments; or even where all your attention is devoted to a single job opportunity at the expense of other promising situations. The fact is, even if everything looks rosy today, nothing in the world is a sure bet. Diversification protects you against downside risk.

IS IT WORTH THE GAMBLE?

People place small bets every day — such as running out to an appointment at the last minute or leaving home without an umbrella. Even though the consequences are small, you're still rolling the dice — sometimes you'll win, other times you'll lose. The danger is that after you get a few wins under your belt, you'll develop a false sense of security and feel you can double down. It's very easy to convince yourself that you're unbeatable. And, like a gambler, your bets get bigger and bigger…until you lose.

Think of the consequences of your actions: What if the big bet doesn't go your way? How would the loss change your life?

So remind me again…why are you risking it all? Is it the thrill and the adrenaline rush? Are you trying to impress your friends?

Living on the edge isn't the "be-all and end-all." It doesn't take a brain surgeon to realize that there are no guarantees in life — which means that playing the odds through excessive risk taking is like playing with fire. Unfortunately, when you get burned, there may be serious consequences. As author Ray Bradbury once said, "Living at risk is jumping off the cliff and building your wings on the way down."

The key, then, is to take calculated risks, and only place bets on things that you're willing to lose. As the saying goes, "Take risks: If you win, you will be happy; if you lose, you will be wise." Make sense? You bet. **:)**

The next time someone says, 'The odds are against you,' remember: If you don't try, you forfeit the opportunity.

THE WINNER'S EDGE

Every day we're bombarded by messages telling us why we can't succeed. "Most companies fail in the first few years." "It didn't work last time." "If it hasn't worked by now, it probably won't." These views can cast serious doubt in our minds. "What are the odds of being successful?" "Why waste the time?" "Why even try?"

Some people treat these words as excuses to stop trying. Winners view these warnings with skepticism — and are determined to prove them wrong.

THE WINNING FORMULA

Believe in yourself. Some people trust others' opinions before heeding their own. There's an urban legend about the flight of bumblebees that's worth repeating.

> One evening at a dinner party in the 1930s, a prominent German aerodynamicist happened to be talking to a biologist, who asked about the flight of bees. To answer the biologist's query, the engineer did a quick "back-of-the-napkin" calculation. He assumed a rigid, smooth wing, estimated the bee's weight and wing area, and calculated the lift generated by the wing. Not surprisingly, there was insufficient lift — he concluded that bumblebees couldn't fly.

If bumblebees listened to the experts, they'd never try to fly. I guess bumble-bees aren't willing to accept that premise.

Don't surrender to naysayers. Every day, people hear broad-based statistics and give up before trying. "It's tough to make a sale this time of the year." "You'll have to wait years to get promoted." "No one has ever achieved that feat before." Rather than view themselves as a possible success story, they adopt a defeatist attitude and give up. The next time someone says, "The odds are against you," remember: If *you* don't try, you forfeit the opportunity.

Accept the possibility of failure. Every opportunity has two potential out-comes — success or failure — with a possible mix in-between. If fear of failure prompts you to forgo opportunities, it becomes a self-fulfilling prophecy — you'll deny yourself the opportunity to succeed. One of the tenets of a winning philosophy is a willingness to accept failure as a possible outcome.

Look for options. Some people hit a wall only to pick themselves up and run into the wall again. Successful people learn from their mistakes and find a way *around* the challenges they face every day. If you hit a wall, find a ladder, or try an end run. Winners look for options.

Be in for the long haul. Some people expect immediate gratification. Unfortunately, they don't realize the commitment and determination required, and they quit, losing everything before reaching the finish line. The truth is, success can't be set to a timetable. It takes many years to become an overnight success.

Get back on your horse. Some folks surrender to failure. Ted Williams, the baseball legend, once commented that those who fail only seven times out of ten attempts will be the greatest in the game. Treat every disappointment as a stepping-stone to success. If you fall off the horse, don't be afraid to get back on again.

Never think one and done. Some folks stop after finding the first acceptable answer. The fact is, our education system too often teaches us that there's only *one* right answer. But your first idea is rarely your best. After you accept that premise, you'll always push yourself to find the best solution.

Leave your comfort zone. Most people seek safety and reassurance by coloring within the lines. The truth is, if you don't stick your neck out, you'll never get ahead. As the saying goes, the only one who likes change is a wet baby.

Make the effort. If you're not willing to make the commitment, don't complain about the outcome. Remember, nothing happens if you don't make it happen. Opportunities, unlike eggs, don't hatch from sitting on them.

WINNERS HAVE THINGS IN COMMON...

Winners recognize the difference between a dream and reality; they exhibit a healthy balance between creating a plan and acting on it; they base decisions on priorities — the things they care about most; and they break major undertakings into small, digestible bites. Winners view obstacles as challenges that can be successfully navigated; they view every small win as a stepping-stone to something bigger and better; and they are humbled by every win, knowing that one win doesn't constitute a winning streak.

Winners aren't always the smartest. They don't always have the greatest experience. They aren't always the best at what they do. But they're passionate, focused, trustworthy, and committed. You can be sure that winners are acquainted with failure, but they're not deterred by it. In fact, winners are unwilling to accept failure as an option. Winners are on a mission! Nothing is going to stand in their way. You can see success in their eyes. They can feel it in their bones. They display a rare sense of optimism that's contagious. Are you a winner? **:)**

If you think you can bluff your way through life, you've got something coming.

BLUFFING YOUR WAY TO THE TOP

Remember the days when you were in school, and studied your tail off for an exam? You found out that one of your classmates, who had partied the night before, blew the socks off the exam because he received the test questions beforehand.

Well, you thought that after you graduated, you left all that baggage behind. Then you found out that these same characters are soaring through the corporate ranks because — you guessed it — they've learned how to "play the system."

Well, I've got a message for these counterfeit superstars: If you think you can bluff your way through life, you've got something coming.

Despite the fact that the majority of people play by the rules, there are a number of bad actors in every organization who advance their careers on the backs of others. Here are eight you may recognize:

Emperors. These people climb the corporate ladder by capitalizing on who they know rather than on what they're contributing. They may have friends in high places, have their walls filled with diplomas, or have previously worked for a blue-chip company. They're like an oasis. They may look wonderful from a distance, but the closer you get, the more obvious it becomes that it's all a mirage. In this case, emperors truly have no clothes.

Pretty Boys (or Girls). These people really look the part. They are the trendiest dressers, belong to the finest country clubs, and look like they could be on the cover of *Vogue* or *GQ*. Similar to Emperors, the Pretty set rise up the corporate ladder based on appearance rather than performance. But their veneer is thin, and when the spotlight gets too bright, you can see right through them. In this case, you shouldn't judge a book simply by its cover.

A-- Kissers. These people spend all their time fawning over their superiors. "You need to reduce costs? No problem. We just won't give people raises this year." (Too bad there's only enough for management.) These A-- Kissers spend 99.9 percent of their time in closed-door management meetings with little time to provide direction for their own team — regardless of the impact that it has on results. In this case, it's only a matter of time before their people say "ENOUGH!" and tell THEM to kiss off.

Delegators. They say there are two kinds of people: those who are willing to work and those who are willing to let them. These counterfeit superstars are in the latter group. They have the power to say, "You want something done? No problem." Then they get their staff to stay late while they leave at 5 p.m. These people always volunteer for more and have the cleanest desks in the office. How's that possible? It's because they delegate everything! In this case, the only thing that stops at their desk is the credit they don't deserve, not the work.

Schmoozers. These folks could win an award for Mr. or Ms. Congeniality. Everybody loves them. Schmoozers know all the ballgame stats; they know how to tell a joke; and they're up-to-date on the inside dirt. Their colleagues like them so much that they don't mind taking on their workload while the schmoozer is entertaining clients elsewhere. In this case, work is a party for schmoozers.

Bystanders. These slouches do just enough to get by. They've been with the organization for a zillion years, rarely speak up, and would make themselves invisible if they could. They spend their day moving piles of paper on their desk while they watch everyone else go crazy trying to get the job done. In fact, when they're out on vacation, nobody even knows they're missing. In this case, the last survivors on Earth, along with cockroaches, will be the bystanders.

Scavengers. These are the types who take the credit for everybody else's work. They surround themselves with talented people and spend the day determining if there's an idea worth stealing — while they fine-tune their personal PR machine. In this case, they'll continue to rise up the company ranks as long as their "credit" remains good.

Busybodies. These individuals spend their whole day trying to prove how busy they are. Whenever they're asked to do something, they spend 20 minutes describing how much work they have on their plate. In this case, if busybodies ever needed a role model, they could look to a turnstile — it's out in front, goes around in circles, creates wind, but never gets anywhere.

Any of these personality types sound familiar? Don't get angry — they'll get their due. They think they're fooling the world, but, sooner or later, everyone catches on to them.

The fact is, by pulling their antics, these counterfeit superstars not only make colleagues row harder to compensate for their deficiencies, they steal the spotlight from very talented people who deserve the recognition. This destroys morale, hurts productivity, and damages competitiveness.

As time goes on, you'll be able to look back on a life marked by honor and self-respect. Meanwhile, these counterfeit superstars will start believing their own press, and they'll get sloppy. Or — ultimately — if they're not caught, they'll meet their match when they run into someone else who beats them at their own game. GOTCHA! **:)**

White lies matter.

THE TRUE COLOR OF WHITE LIES

magine having this conversation about white lies with your conscience:

Conscience: "Are you really going to tell a white lie, break a promise, or stretch the truth?"

"Oh come on," you answer. "You're not going to judge me, are you? It's 'just this one time.' White lies never hurt anyone. Everyone does it. Besides, I never said I was a saint."

Sound familiar?

THE TRUTH ABOUT WHITE LIES

I'm sure everyone has a "good" excuse for telling a white lie. "It's for my family." "I want to protect her feelings." "It's for the good of the organization." But here's the rub…

The first time you tell a lie, break a promise, or stretch the truth, you'll probably give it some thought — weighing the advantages and disadvantages of lowering your personal standards. You'll undoubtedly be a little nervous because your conscience told you not to do it, but you decided to go that route anyway. And, if you get away with it, you may even think you won, but did you?

The next time you're faced with a similar situation, you'll probably give it less thought than the first time, and you may even accept a little more risk. Before you know it, you'll undoubtedly think you can get away with telling lies every time. Why not? The score is already two for you and zero for your conscience. You may become so accustomed to fibbing that you don't even question how much you've lowered the bar for yourself.

WHITE LIES MATTER

You can try to convince me that you're right, if that makes you feel better, but I choose to live my life the right way. Folks like me know that when we make a promise, our word is as binding as a contract. And we know that there's no reason for someone to challenge our word or second-guess our motives — because we live our life with honor and integrity. That enables us to build trust, strengthen credibility and respect, and earn a solid reputation. What's that worth? Everything!

Some people may argue that the world isn't black and white. They know how close they can go "to the edge" so there's no danger of this downward spiral. Well, that's a decision between them and their conscience.

As for others, they can explain their actions away by saying that "everyone does it" or they're doing it for the "right reason." But I question whether they're trying to persuade others or to convince themselves.

So the next time you find yourself saying "just this one time," remember what you're trading off in the process. Forget about what you may lose from your friends and colleagues, and start thinking about whether you'll be able to face yourself in the mirror every day. Is it worth it? You'll have to answer that for yourself. My only advice is to listen to your conscience. That's why you have one. **:)**

When you make a promise, you're not giving your word in erasable pencil, you're inscribing your commitment in indelible ink.

DO YOU TAKE YOUR COMMITMENTS SERIOUSLY?

We make commitments every day. They can be simple or life-changing — from simply promising to complete a task to making a lifelong commitment such as becoming a parent or asking for someone's hand in marriage. But do we take our commitments seriously? Commitment is one of those things that some people do without thinking while others never think of doing.

Some folks make commitments at the drop of a hat, thinking they can walk away from the obligation if they change their mind. Don't they understand that commitments come with responsibility? Don't they care that they may be hurting someone they care about? Don't they understand that their actions have consequences? If the answer is yes, why don't people honor their commitments?

BROKEN PROMISES, BROKEN COMMITMENTS

Commitments often fail because people:

Lack personal responsibility. Some people make commitments too easily. Then, as soon as the wind changes direction, they head for the exit.

Make a minimal commitment. Some folks are afraid of getting hurt so they dip their toe in the water rather than jumping in.

Play the field. Some people don't like to be tied down. They'd rather settle for several superficial relationships than one meaningful one.

"Jump ship" for a better offer. Some folks are opportunists. They're always on the prowl for a better situation.

Look out for number one. Some people are strictly out for themselves. These selfish folks have a hard time making a commitment that requires even minimal sacrifice.

Keep score. Some folks treat a relationship as a competition. They can't stand being on the losing end, even for a short period of time.

Make too many commitments. Some people can't find the words or courage to decline a request. They end up breaking their promise; one that they never felt comfortable about making from the start.

"Chicken out" during tough times. Some people have no character. As soon as something goes south, they're nowhere to be found.

DO YOU UNDERSTAND THE MEANING OF COMMITMENT?

Here are nine ingredients of a successful commitment. Use them as guideposts through your life.

Go all in. Think twice before making a commitment. Once you do, take the plunge rather than making a half-hearted effort.

Honor your word. Accept responsibility. When you make a commitment, you're giving your word and putting your honor on the line. Act like it.

Expect the best. Put your complete trust and faith in the commitments that you make. That will encourage you to focus on long-term potential rather than seeking immediate gain.

Keep the relationship front and center. Focus as much on the journey as on the end result. Never sacrifice the relationship for results.

Give first. Give with an open hand. The odds are high that your deed will be reciprocated. But remember, there's no need to keep score.

Make yourself vulnerable. Be honest and transparent. That will promote a healthy, trusting relationship.

Demonstrate your loyalty. Live up to your commitments in good times and bad. Tough times say a lot about us. Make sure they say only good things about you.

Watch each other's back. Promote opportunities where everyone wins. Focus on their best interests and have faith that they'll focus on yours.

Think as one. Build together, grow together, and win together. It's that simple.

IS YOUR COMMITMENT AS BINDING AS A CONTRACT?

People are way too quick to make commitments and too quick to abandon them. When you make a commitment, you're not saying I'll give it a shot, you're saying, I'm all in — and nothing less. When you make a commitment, you're not saying you've got more than I've got, you're saying I'm so happy that you're happy. When you make a commitment, you're not saying I'll honor my responsibility when times are good, you're saying count on me to be at my best when times are worst. The truth is, when you make a promise, you're not giving your word in erasable pencil, you're inscribing your commitment in indelible ink.

Making a commitment is serious business and not something to be taken lightly. When you make a commitment, you're not *only* keeping your commitment for *their* benefit, you're also keeping it for yourself. That's because your honor and self-respect hang in the balance. What's that worth? Everything! Be very careful about making commitments and always be faithful in keeping them. **:)**

Knowing what's right
isn't as important as
doing what's right.

LIVE WITH HONOR AND INTEGRITY

S ome people try to appear honorable in order to win the admiration of others. Although this may be true, they have it all backward. The real benefit of being honorable isn't in how others view you, but rather, in how you view yourself. When you live with integrity, you don't have to worry about inconsistencies, remember what you said to whom, or play games. There's no need to fear embarrassment, no need to hide in the shadows or to live in shame. When you live with honor, you're comfortable in your skin and totally authentic. As former Senator Alan K. Simpson said, "If you have integrity, nothing else matters. If you don't have integrity, nothing else matters."

12 WAYS TO LIVE WITH HONOR AND INTEGRITY

People with honor share 12 characteristics. They should be treated as guide-posts in your journey through life:

Value integrity. Recognize who you are and the values that you aspire to. Provide others with the confidence of knowing that your intentions and actions are always genuine. Be prepared to compromise your viewpoint, but never your principles.

Be true to yourself. In staying true to your beliefs, be sure to do right by others and to always take the high ground. Trust your instincts rather than seeking validation from others. You have to live with yourself for the rest of your life.

Keep good company. Surround yourself with honorable people. Support each other. Allow them to serve as role models and sounding boards that inspire you to become a better you. And look for ways to help others grow in honor and integrity.

Be confident. Don't let your behavior be influenced by others who do not share your values; hold yourself to a much higher standard — your conscience. Your character is on display every moment of every day. Make sure it reflects well on you and causes people to feel proud to call you a friend.

Do what's right. Make good choices. Follow the spirit as well as the letter of the law. At the center of the United States Military Academy is the Cadet Honor Code, which states "A Cadet will not lie, cheat, steal, or tolerate those who do." Care not only about where life is taking you, but about how you're getting there as well.

Be honest and transparent. When you stand for honesty, everything you say carries the voice of credibility. But when you're dishonest, your soiled reputation will do the speaking for you. The fact is, honest people never fear the truth.

Honor your word. Every time you make a promise, you put your honor and integrity on the line. Keeping that promise *should* be as important to you as it is to the recipient.

Be loyal. Meaningful relationships don't happen by chance. When you live with honor, people know your behavior is reliable, your heart is in the right place, and your word is as good as gold.

Accept personal responsibility. Be prepared to accept the consequences of your actions. Knowing what's right isn't as important as doing what's right. Be aware that yours will not always be the most popular road traveled.

Be resilient. Hard work and sacrifice build character, contribute to success, and promote happiness. It was this very reality that moved former baseball player Sam Ewing to observe, "Hard work spotlights the character of people: some turn up their sleeves, some turn up their noses, and some don't turn up at all."

Make a difference. Be a positive force in people's lives. Make people feel special; bring out the best in them; help them without expecting something in return; be genuinely happy for their achievements. The more you do for others, the happier you'll be.

Live for a cause greater than yourself. Find your life's purpose. It will inspire you, keep you grounded, and provide stability regardless of the turbulence in your life. Most of all, living life with purpose will motivate you to get up in the morning and make your life meaningful.

DO YOURSELF THE HONOR

There'll come a time when temptation will come knocking at your door. It'll promise you riches or something equally as grand. Don't surrender. If it's too good to be true, it probably is. It's sad to say that some people will give in to a moment of weakness and spend the rest of their lives regretting it. They'll rationalize the situation by thinking "What are the odds of getting caught?" Or they'll say, "Everybody does it," "It's only one time" to help them sleep better at night.

But the question remains, what is your honor worth to you? The answer is that it's priceless. What's more valuable than being able to look into the mirror each day with a clear conscience? As the author H. Jackson Brown, Jr., said, "Live so that when your children think of fairness, caring, and integrity, they think of you." Equally important is that *you* will respect *yourself*. One of the true tests of integrity is your refusal to compromise your honor at any price. Can your integrity be bought? **:)**

Ask yourself whether the problem will matter in a year or two. If not, it may be a trivial issue unworthy of your concern.

HOW HEAVY IS YOUR BAGGAGE?

Imagine carrying a backpack, filled with rocks, everywhere you go. If that seems like too much to bear, imagine the weight of the emotional baggage that we carry every day! Think about it…we *fear* getting fired, we *complain* about the service we receive, we *envy* the person "next door," we *worry* about meeting deadlines, and we *mistrust* our colleague for "stealing" the promotion. Emotional baggage? You bet.

Now ask yourself: What do we gain by ranting or working ourselves up into a tizzy? Answer: We get ourselves all upset, with little to show for our efforts. The truth is, besides being a colossal waste of time, nothing really changes — except that we're not much fun to be around. Who needs that?

Even when we don't overtly express our negative feelings of revenge, anger, prejudice, fear, criticism, guilt, worry, and envy, we play out these "dramas" in our heads. These negative thoughts race through our minds like a whirlwind, making us more and more anxious each time we revisit them. In fact, some people get so overwhelmed that they work themselves into a frenzy, making it tough to concentrate during the day and causing sleep issues at night. Taken to the extreme, emotional baggage can be absolutely debilitating if not controlled. *It's important to note that mental health is a real concern. People who are unable to deal with their issues are advised to seek professional support.*

The bottom line is that these "emotional tirades" are unproductive, unhealthy, and draining. No wonder we're exhausted.

TAKE A LOAD OFF YOUR MIND

Here are six suggestions to reduce your emotional baggage that masquerades as revenge, worry, prejudice, fear, criticism, guilt, anger, and envy.

Food for thought. One of the first steps that people take when trying to lose weight is to write down the food they eat each day. Seeing it in writing represents an important motivator toward changing eating habits. In the same way, by listing the negative thoughts that cross our minds each day, we can use the food technique to reduce our emotional baggage.

Keep it positive. Negative thinking isn't always bad. In fact, having some fear and worry keeps you on your toes, forces you to prepare *early*, and encourages you to anticipate future events by asking yourself, what if? On the other hand, when emotional baggage makes you angry, increases your anxiety, or overwhelms you, it's a negative to avoid.

Is that a fact? It's very helpful to determine whether the assumptions behind your fears, worries, prejudices, etc., are factual and realistic. When you're tired, emotional, or under stress, negative thoughts can spiral out of control and ruin your day, even if the premise behind your anxiety is far-fetched. That's a fact.

The sky is falling! How often do your fears and worries actually come true? If they rarely come to fruition, why are you getting all worked up? Odds are that you'd have a better chance of getting hit by lightning.

Make it happen. Many fears are beyond our control. Therefore, if a problem wakes you up at 3 a.m., and you can do something about it, even at that hour, do it. If not, forget about it and go to sleep. If it's truly beyond your control, then all your worry and sleeplessness won't change the situation. Put the worry behind you and move on.

Will it even matter? Some situations appear larger than life, yet in hindsight they seem inconsequential. The key is to gauge the issue beforehand. As a simple test, ask yourself whether the problem will matter in a year or two. If not, it may be a trivial issue unworthy of your concern.

BREAK FREE FROM YOUR BAGGAGE

It's unfair and unrealistic to think it's easy to unpack the emotional baggage that we've accumulated over a lifetime — but that shouldn't stop us from trying. If Buddha's words are true, "What we think, we become," then it's vital to take control of our lives.

Our fears are often worse than reality. We worry about impressing our friends, when the truth is that *real* friends remain by our side in good times and bad. We worry about being late for a meeting. If we are, it won't change mankind. We also get angry waiting at home all day for a delivery person. And that too shall pass.

The truth is, in most cases, life goes on. You have the power to make yourself happy or miserable during your life journey. There are very few times in life when we hit a wall so hard that we don't recover from it. We pick ourselves up, dust ourselves off, and move on. The difference is, if you take a pledge to be positive, and start reducing your emotional baggage, you're going to lead a happier, healthier, more fulfilling life. As Norman Vincent Peale once said, "Change your thoughts and you change your world." **:)**

There are simply
no shortcuts in
the long run.

EASY STREET IS FILLED WITH POTHOLES

Some folks buy pills to lose weight, go under the knife to look young, and purchase lottery tickets in hopes of striking it rich. In business, they request favors five minutes into a new relationship, hold "fire sales" rather than building customer loyalty, and bark orders at employees rather than leading with trust. They believe (or should I say, hope) that taking the quick-and-easy route is the optimum path to success.

The problem is, if you think trust, respect, and credibility are easy to obtain, you're kidding yourself. If you think loyalty is created, a reputation is earned, or success is achieved at the drop of a hat, you're sadly mistaken. And if you think money can buy youth, gifts can win a child's love, and a clean bill of health can be attained without healthy living, you're dreaming. In fact, if you think there's a magic bullet for anything worthwhile in life, you're living a fantasy. Success requires hard work, commitment, patience, and determination. There are simply no shortcuts in the long run.

THERE ARE NO SHORTCUTS TO SUCCESS

Here are common examples in which taking the easy route sabotages our long-term success:

In our personal life:

- We measure relationships by what we've *gained* rather than by what we've *done* to strengthen the bond.

- We negotiate agreements to gain the upper hand rather than making everything win-win.

- We address easy items on our to-do list rather than tackling more challenging priorities that require immediate attention.

- We view new acquaintances as opportunities, ripe for the taking, and then wonder why networking fails.

- We retain attorneys and PR machines to defend ourselves rather than living honorably in the first place.

- We buy things to feed our ego and then face crushing bills that we can ill afford.

In business:

- We chase new business opportunities while letting dissatisfied customers slip through the cracks.

- We're too busy to mentor new hires and then wonder why these talented folks are slow to learn the ropes.

- We settle for the first answer rather than exploring all possible options.

- We squeeze vendors into submission and then expect their loyalty.

- We terminate employees without regard to the impact on the survivors.

- We maximize quarterly performance at the expense of a promising future.

YOUR FUTURE IS NOW

Tomorrow's coming whether you're ready or not. People who don't anticipate the future often seem surprised when it arrives — and it usually does. So plan ahead. But remember that thinking about tomorrow isn't the same as *doing* something about it.

You must plant seeds to reap a harvest. As the Chinese proverb says, "The best time to plant a tree was 20 years ago. The second best time is now." So sacrifice today to secure your future. But make sure to strike a balance…short-term wins enable you to build trust, instill confidence, and maintain momentum.

Don't swing for the fences. While hitting singles may not be as exciting as hitting home runs, they both put points on the board. Plus, the cumulative impact of doing small things in a consistent and dependable manner is huge. So don't belittle the small things that you do each day. As Frank A. Clark, the politician, once said, "Everyone is trying to accomplish something big, not realizing that life is made up of little things."

There's no shortcut to success. Nothing great was ever achieved without desire, hard work, and sacrifice. If the grass is greener on the other side of the fence, chances are it's getting better care.

Whether you're trying to establish credibility, develop a trusting relationship, adopt a healthy lifestyle, or build a reputation, don't expect to hit pay dirt overnight. Easy street is filled with potholes. Be patient. Create milestones to measure your progress, and whatever you do, live with honor. People with integrity inspire credibility, instill confidence, encourage respect, and are able to hold their head high. That itself is a great reward. Plus, doing things for the right reason will come back to you in spades. The key to success is knowing that your situation today is often determined by your choices and actions yesterday. As Aesop said, "Slow and steady wins the race." Long-term outlook. Hard work. Patience. Honor. Now that's a winning formula. **:)**

It's not that there's
not enough time…
the time needed
was spent doing
something else.

THERE'S NO DRESS REHEARSAL IN LIFE

" She called me a bad name." "He took my toy." "She didn't like my dress." "I had it first." Ah yes, the thrill of being young again. Remember how important these things seemed when we were young children? In retrospect, they seem so trivial.

Of course, as we get older and wiser, we focus on important things, like showing our friends how successful we've become, outflanking our colleagues to get a promotion, keeping up with the Joneses, and ensuring that we look young — forever. You'd think we'd have learned something from our kindergarten days, wouldn't you?

The truth is, we're so busy running on our treadmill to nowhere that we lose focus on the things that really matter. Before we know it, the seconds become minutes, the days become weeks, and the months become years. And when we finally take time to catch our breath, we look back and think, "Where did all the time go?"

It's so easy to be blinded by ambition, power, and success that many folks miss out on the simple pleasures of life. Now, I know that you lead a hectic life and that you're getting pulled in a million different directions. Every time you focus on one thing in your life, you've also decided not to spend that time doing something else. The truth is, it's not that there's not enough time…the time needed was spent doing something else. So, if you regret the path you're on, it's time to change course.

Here are five guideposts to point you in the right direction:

Priorities. Have you ever stopped to think about what matters most to you? Do you spend the majority of your time in those areas? Or do trivial issues sidetrack you?

Agenda. Do you let other people control your agenda? How much time do you spend reacting to fire drills?

Time management. Do you devote more time thinking about your to-do list or to making things happen? When was the last time you identified and eliminated wasteful tasks and routines to free up time for your priorities?

Quality. What percentage of your time are you physically present, but mentally absent? How much of your day is spent worrying about problems versus appreciating the moment? Does multitasking damage your ability to give your undivided attention?

Inner peace. Do you care more about what you want out of life or about what others want from you?

THE DECISION IS YOURS

It's so easy to get caught up in the day-to-day minutiae that we lose sight of the big picture.

Even those who have secured enviable positions of power and material wealth admit that these paths have come with real costs — in relationships and precious moments that can't be replaced. This doesn't have to be you.

The path that you choose is your decision and yours alone. The only correct answer is the one that feels best for you. As George Eliot, the English author, once said, "It is never too late to be what you might have been." The key is to establish goals that matter most to you and your loved ones, align your priorities around these goals, and then pursue them, while remaining true to yourself and to those who love you.

Your goal shouldn't be cramming as much stuff as possible into your life. (You'd think we'd learn something from watching a hamster run around on its wheel.) Success and happiness are achieved by focusing your attention in areas that matter most to you. No matter how old you are, you still have time to change course. As the author Alan Lakein once said, "Time = Life, Therefore, waste your time and waste of your life, or master your time and master your life." Are you spending your precious time in areas that matter most to you? There's no dress rehearsal in life. :)

"

Having kids is not
the same as being
a parent.

"

PARENTHOOD ISN'T CHILD'S PLAY

Parenthood is one of the most rewarding experiences in life. There's nothing like watching your kids grow up to be principled human beings living up to their potential. But even though this aspiration seems to be realistic and noble, getting them across the finish line isn't always easy. That's because parenthood isn't child's play.

Unlike the change of seasons, raising good kids doesn't happen as a matter of course. Furthermore, you can't buy a magic pill or delegate the responsibility to others. You make it happen.

If you want your kids to grow up to be happy, successful, and well-adjusted adults, it requires time, dedication, and love (with a touch of luck). Furthermore, while teachers and religious leaders can help reinforce the values that you hold dear, the responsibility lies solely with you. The truth is, having kids is not the same as being a parent.

16 TIPS FOR BEING A GREAT PARENT

It's a parent's responsibility to raise kids who have strong morals and who will be productive members of society.

Here are 16 things that parents can do to raise great kids:

Make your children feel loved. Show affection. Make them safe and secure.

Be a part of your children's lives. Be available and involved. Spend quality time with your children, alone, and as a family. When kids are ready to talk, be ready to listen.

Build confidence. Be your children's biggest cheerleader. Help them develop self-esteem and self-reliance through active guidance and nurturing.

Shape character. Teach your children the difference between right and wrong. Use real-life experiences to build and reinforce moral character, personal values, and self-sufficiency.

Promote basic values. Teach your kids to: share, tell the truth, play fair, keep their promises, have faith, do their best, pull their weight, show kindness and respect, remember their manners, help the less fortunate, kiss and make up, value each other's opinion, learn from mistakes, bounce back from failure, practice what they preach, stick together, listen before they talk, clean up their own mess, have each other's back, be a good friend, and put family first.

Inspire good habits. Set high expectations. Encourage habits that promote good health, happiness, and success.

Support the importance of education. Encourage curiosity while stressing the importance of continuous improvement and lifelong learning.

Teach life skills. Impart critical life skills such as good study and organization routines, time management, planning ahead, problem solving, selling an idea, multitasking, giving and receiving feedback, basic budgeting and financial management, healthy living and nutrition, personal safety, home repairs and maintenance, personal hygiene, manners, and mental health.

Give unconditional love. Celebrate wins and offer a shoulder to cry on when times are tough.

Know how your children are being influenced. Know where your children are, and with whom, and how they're using social media.

Encourage personal responsibility. With freedom comes responsibility. Teach your children that they are accountable for their words and actions.

Show some discipline. Be tough, but fair. Positive and negative reinforcement should be timely and consistent. Remember, if we don't address poor behavior, we're encouraging it through our inaction.

Be a great role model. Demonstrate the importance of living with honor and integrity through your words and actions. As Robert Fulghum, the author, said, "Don't worry that children never listen to you; worry that they are always watching you."

Celebrate traditions. Tradition offers an excellent context for meaningful pause and reflection. It provides an excellent forum to showcase role models and celebrate the things that really matter in life.

Be optimistic and hopeful. When kids grow up, they hear their parent's voice in their subconscious. Teach your kids that they can achieve their dreams as long as they work hard, do what's right, and put their mind to it.

Clarify life's journey. Teach your kids the difference between success and happiness and help them live a purposeful life.

PARENTHOOD ISN'T A SPECTATOR SPORT

Being a good parent isn't for the faint of heart. It'll test your wisdom, challenge your stamina, and defy your patience. But even though you're not financially compensated for being on your toes 24/7, it's the most rewarding job in the world.

Being a parent is the gift that keeps on giving. You put your heart into raising your children and are rewarded every day — by watching them grow into good and loving adults. But don't kid yourself…there are many ways this train can go off the tracks. That's where you come in. Kids require time and attention. Meeting those needs isn't a gift of the wealthy, but of the caring. Nothing you do for your children is ever wasted. The truth is, behind all good kids are parents or caregivers who understand the importance of raising them that way. As Frederick Douglass, the orator and statesman, said, "It's easier to build strong children than to repair broken men." Our future is dependent on our kids. And the future of your children is dependent on you. Parenthood isn't child's play. Are you doing your part? **:)**

Life is a classroom.

A NEW SCHOOL
OF THOUGHT

You went to a prominent school and graduated with honors. So you're set for life. Right? Well…not so fast. Unfortunately, there may be a gaping hole in your education so large that you could drive a truck through it. The fact is, while you may have a diploma, a piece of paper doesn't guarantee success.

Let's see…you took all the required courses in school, such as math, English, social studies, science, foreign language, the humanities, etc. Have we forgotten anything?

I don't know how to break this to you, but your employer isn't going to announce a pop quiz and hand you a blue book on your first day of work. You'll be expected to solve real problems rather than answering multiple-choice questions. In fact, you'll be asked to think critically, make tough decisions, and juggle several projects at the same time.

YOU THINK YOU'RE SO SMART

It's no secret that the first requirement for success is **Completing School**. If you don't finish school or learn a trade, you'll be facing headwinds for the rest of your life.

The second requirement for success is obtaining a good skill set. **Foundation Skills** enable you to apply the knowledge that you've learned. Examples include, but are not limited to:

Problem solving • Decision making • Interpersonal communication • Giving and receiving feedback • Critical/analytical thinking • Multitasking • Collaboration/teamwork • Written and oral communication • Interviewing • Networking • Cross-cultural sensitivity • Self-directed learning • Digital literacy • Time management • Negotiating

The third requirement for success is embracing sound beliefs and values. **Core Values** serve as guiding principles for your behavior. Examples include, but are not limited to:

Be positive • Practice what you preach • Do yourself proud • Meet others halfway • Work hard, work smart • Sacrifice for the good of the team • Play fair • Make it win-win • Bring out the best in others • Remain loyal • Keep an open mind • Never quit • Do right by others • Be self-reliant • Tell the truth • Learn through life • Make a difference • Do the right thing • Live with honor • Be a good winner and loser

The fourth requirement for success is strong **Moral Character**. The qualities that comprise moral character define you as a person. The truth is, nothing will propel or destroy a promising career faster than the presence or absence of moral character. Period! You are expected to be:

Honest and trustworthy • Straightforward and transparent • Ethical and principled • Authentic • Determined • Accountable • Self-sufficient • Fair and open-minded • Consistent and dependable • Passionate • Confident and optimistic • Empathetic and selfless • Humble • Proud • Courageous • Ambitious • Hardworking

The fifth requirement for success is being able to manage your personal life effectively — **Living 101**. It's difficult, if not impossible, to compartmentalize your life — your home life will affect your work life and vice versa. It's important to acquire knowledge in the following areas:

Managing a home • Searching for a job • Balancing a checkbook • Taking out a car loan • Purchasing insurance • Investing • Parenting • Work-life balance • Healthy living • Nutrition • Stress management • Tax planning • Fitness • Basic car maintenance • Retirement planning • Manners and etiquette

GET SMART: LEARN A THING OR TWO (OR MAYBE THREE)

The obvious question is: "Is a formal education everything it's cracked up to be?" The simple answer is yes, BUT being book smart is only a start. If you're greedy, ruthless, and lazy, you're lost before you even begin. If you can't communicate, play nice with people, or manage your time effectively, you'll never get out of the starting gate. If you're careless, unreliable, or dishonest, you're cooked. And if your home life is inadequate, you're in for a rude awakening if you think your work life won't suffer as a result. Going to school teaches you *some* of what you need to know, but it's your job to acquire the rest.

There are three requirements to achieve success in work. First, you must be qualified to secure a job. Second, you must have the knowledge, skills, personal values, and moral character to perform your job well. Last, but not least, while self-directed learning doesn't come with a choking tuition bill, success does require desire and determination. As Andrew Carnegie said, "You cannot push anyone up the ladder unless he is willing to climb."

The fact is, life is a classroom. After graduation, *you* determine what to learn, when the learning will take place, and how to tailor it to your personal needs. There will be no forced curriculum, no required exams, and no grades — except the ones you give yourself. Your only test will be how much you can learn and apply to your daily life. There won't be a person cracking a whip. There won't be a spotlight highlighting the life lesson. And if you decide this isn't for you, no one may ever know — but it will be your loss. So broaden your world, open your mind to new horizons, connect the dots, request feedback, question routines, break bad habits, learn from mistakes, critique your actions, mimic role models, and challenge yourself. You'll find that every experience offers a life lesson. As the actor Will Smith said, "The things that have been most valuable to me I did not learn in school." So open your eyes to the world around you and set the world on fire. If you follow this path, the smart money will be on you. **:)**

"

Trust is like blood
pressure. It's silent,
vital to good health,
and if abused,
it can be deadly.

"

TRUST ME ...
TRUST ME NOT!

Trust is the fabric that binds us together, creating an orderly, civilized society from chaos and anarchy. If we can't trust our husband or our wife, if we can't trust our children, if we can't trust our boss or our colleagues, if we can't trust our religious leader or our senator, then we have nothing on which to build a stable way of life. Trust is not an abstract, theoretical, idealistic goal forever beyond our reach. Trust — or a lack of it — is inherent in every action that we take and affects everything that we do. Trust is the cement that binds relationships, keeping spouses together, business deals intact, and political systems stable. Without trust, marriages fail, voters become apathetic, and organizations flounder. The fact is, without trust, no company can ever hope for excellence.

Trust is like love in a marriage: it bonds people together and makes them strong and effective. Trust in a relationship increases security, reduces inhibitions and defensiveness, and frees people to share feelings and dreams. Trust empowers you to put your deepest fears in the palms of your colleagues' hands, knowing that they will be treated with care. Trust enables you to be yourself and maintain your own values without worrying about acceptance. Trust makes people willing to spend time together and make sacrifices for one another. Trust is an expression of faith that makes it easy for colleagues to have confidence in one another's ability to perform well and to know that they will be there if needed. Trust means that promises made will be kept, and it also means that if a promise is not kept, it was probably for good cause. And finally, trust means that a relationship will last not because something is expected in return, but because the relationship itself is valued.

There has, however, been a deep, fundamental change in the way we view the world today, and as a result, trust is no longer fashionable. Few adults can remember a world without cynicism. Where "death do us part" once had meaning, today one of two new marriages ends in divorce, and countless others exist in name only. Politicians who were once solid members of the community are defaming their office due to scandals and irregularities. Employees who once believed in devoting their entire working lives to one organization have seen so many colleagues tossed out in restructurings and outsourcings that those who remain are often left emotionally uninvolved in their jobs.

The trust deficit is a sea change from the time when a friend's word was his bond; when employees worked for one company until they retired; when business deals were made on the basis of "I know your family" or "We've worked with your company before." These were all ways of saying we recognize your values, understand how much your reputation means to you, and know how you choose to live your life. These values resulted in strong communication, loyal friendships, and increased business.

If businesses are to thrive in the global marketplace, trust must be more than something that is talked about; it must be at the core of everything that is done. Organizations cannot be jungles where only the fittest survive, living in a state of battle readiness in order to meet the grueling tests of everyday corporate life. Trust must be present in everything we do. The bottom line is that trust is like blood pressure. It's silent, vital to good health, and if abused, it can be deadly. **:)**

Moments, rather than possessions, are the true treasures of life.

MOMENTS LOST

One minute doesn't seem like much over a lifetime, but even a second matters more than you think. The fact is, precious moments pass in the blink of an eye. And once they're gone, they're gone forever.

It's so easy to get overwhelmed by the complexities of life. We juggle a million balls, run in a zillion directions, and respond to demands that are placed on us each day. The result is that we're so busy being busy that we allow ourselves to get distracted from the things that really matter.

WHERE DID TIME GO?

Are you conscious of the habits you've developed over time?

Busy bee. Some people are always on the run. They spend so much time looking at their watch that they rarely take time to savor the moment.

Worrywart. Some folks are so afraid of what tomorrow will bring that they spend more time worrying about what *might* happen than enjoying what *is* happening.

Juggler. Some people multitask so much that they never give their undivided attention to anything. Even though they're physically present, you're never quite sure if they're *really* there.

Naysayer. Some folks are so busy complaining about life that they fail to see the rainbow shining through the clouds.

Braggart. Some people are so fixated on showing off their success that they don't realize their game-playing is all-consuming — with no end in sight.

Eager beaver. Some folks' lust for power starts out as a goal, but ends up as an obsession. They're so busy clawing their way to the top that they overlook the price they're paying to get there.

Hothead. Some people spend so much time harboring anger that it consumes their day and overshadows their blessings.

Ungrateful. Some folks take things for granted and then frantically try to win back what they never took the time to appreciate.

Pushover. Some people spend so much effort trying to win acceptance from others that they never satisfy their own needs.

Grouch. Some folks bring work concerns home with them and take their frustrations out on the people they care about most.

Self-absorbed. Some people are so wrapped up in their own needs that they fail to notice the desires of their loved ones.

Time waster. Some folks waste their time each day and then wonder, with amazement, why they don't have time for anything that's important to them.

NOT A MOMENT TO SPARE

If some of these habits sound familiar to you, it's time to chart a new course. Here are eight points to keep in mind.

Develop good habits. It's just as easy to develop a good habit as a bad habit. So be conscious of your actions and scrutinize your behavior — remember that repetition often becomes habit.

Prioritize. Keep a proper perspective. Everything on your plate isn't equally important. Checking items off a to-do list doesn't determine progress; focus your attention on the things that matter.

Invest your time. Think of time as your most valuable currency and invest it wisely.

Think small. Although most people plan for major milestones, it's equally important to recognize the small things. Over time, the cumulative effect of doing the little things right, each and every day, makes a BIG difference.

Do one thing at a time. Try to focus on one thing at a time. When you feel the urge to multitask, pull yourself back.

Disconnect. Every call, text, or e-mail doesn't require an immediate response. Disconnect and enjoy the moment. Things will wait.

Do nothing. Life doesn't have to be a race. Spend some time doing nothing and enjoying the silence and solitude.

Live in the moment. Yesterday is over and tomorrow may never happen. Plan for tomorrow, but live for today.

MOMENTS DON'T LAST FOREVER

When I look around I see so many folks scrambling to meet life's growing demands. What do we gain, or lose, by acting this way? The truth is, it's so easy to get caught up in our routines that we don't realize we're turning life into a race. (You'd think we'd learn something from watching a hamster run around on its wheel.) Wouldn't it be unfortunate if you opened your eyes one day and sighed, "I should have" — when you actually could have?

One day you'll recognize how valuable special moments were in your life. You'll appreciate the joy that those times brought you in the past and the pleasure their memories bring you today. And you'll realize that moments, rather than possessions, are the true treasures of life. In fact, you wouldn't trade them for all the riches in the world. So, if you can't "find" the time to quit the rat race…make the time! Seize each moment before it passes you by. Remember, moments don't last forever, but their memories do. **:)**

Achieving success is hard; staying successful is even harder.

COMPLACENCY: THE ENEMY OF SUCCESS

You've worked hard to achieve success. You've struggled through hard times, you've met challenges head on, and you've fought the hard battles. You've finally reached the pinnacle of success. But you're about to face your toughest challenge yet — complacency. Achieving success is hard; staying successful is even harder.

COMPLACENCY: THE SILENT KILLER

Are you in danger of becoming complacent? Here are nine warning signs that signal trouble ahead for you or your business. If you:

Take success for granted. Some folks become complacent and coast. They fool themselves into believing that their comfortable lead can't be lost.

Lose focus. Some folks abandon the things that made them successful. They drift away from what they know and do best.

Fail to learn. Some folks are so busy celebrating success they fail to notice that the world around them is changing — and they're not keeping up with the times.

Stop listening. Some folks let success go to their head. They think they know everything — and no one has the courage to tell them otherwise.

Fight for attention. Some folks forget that success was a team effort and try to steal the spotlight. This causes ill will and resentment among all the team members.

Go on defense. Some folks go on defense thinking the "game" is already won. They react to situations rather than pursuing opportunities.

Lose sense of pride. Some folks lose their passion and get careless.

Believe in a sense of entitlement. Some folks believe past success guarantees future success. They want the rewards without the hard work.

Ignore the customer. You know a business is complacent when it piles up costs that don't add customer value; when it develops policy changes for employee convenience rather than for customer benefit; when it spends more time in staff meetings than in front of customers; when it protects its existing installations rather than developing great new products for customers.

COMPLACENCY: DON'T FALL ASLEEP AT THE WHEEL

You're at the top of your game. It appears nothing is going to stop you — except you. Here are twelve ways to fight complacency:

Don't let your guard down. Give yourself a kick in the butt. If you're not up to the job, find someone who is.

Stay grounded. Remember what made you successful and what you've learned along the way.

Create stretch goals. Push your limits. Set ambitious yet realistic goals. Challenge everyone to do better and to be better. The fact is, if you spend your life coasting, it'll all be downhill.

Don't be a know-it-all. Know what you know and what you don't know. It's strength, not weakness, to seek advice from others.

Welcome fresh ideas. Invite fresh new thinking that challenges your perspective. The truth is, surrounding yourself with yes people is like talking to yourself.

Learn from the best. Never stop growing. Identify best practices and make sure to implement them.

Compete with yourself. View success as a journey rather than as a destination. Focus on beating your best rather than your competition. That way you'll always be growing and learning from the best in the field — yourself.

Fight against routine. Embrace change. If it ain't broke, break it.

Look for areas of vulnerability. Ask "what-if" questions to uncover blind spots. Be your own customer. Find the cracks in your system.

Never underestimate the opposition. Wake up. Any military strategist will tell you that underestimating the enemy is courting defeat.

Maintain momentum. Don't let up. As soon as you achieve one goal, set another. It's easier to maintain momentum than to rebuild it once it's lost.

Look to the future (not the past). Take the time to smell the roses, but don't spend too much time basking in the glory of success. As Andrew Grove, former CEO of Intel, said, "Success breeds complacency. Complacency breeds failure. Only the paranoid survive."

COMPLACENCY: CONTROL IT BEFORE IT CONTROLS YOU

Wherever you find success you'll find complacency. But you have the ability to control your situation — if you have the will and desire. It takes so much to become successful, why bring yourself down? As Benjamin E. Mays, the minister and educator, said, "The tragedy of life is often not in our failure, but rather in our complacency; not in our doing too much, but rather in our doing too little; not in our living above our ability, but rather in our living below our capacities." Don't look over your shoulder to see who's coming; the real opposition lies with yourself. Complacency is the enemy of success. **:)**

"

You send a message by what you say and what you do. If words aren't supported with consistent actions, they will ring hollow.

"

ACTIONS SPEAK LOUDER THAN WORDS

The car with a religious bumper sticker just cut me off. The parent makes the rules and then routinely breaks them. The leader just asked everyone to scale back and then spends like there's no tomorrow. The politician says, "Trust me," but we quickly learn that his promises are empty. The truth is, talk is cheap. Actions speak louder than words.

Why do people say one thing and do another? Why do they make promises one second only to break them minutes later? Why do people say they care when it's so obvious they couldn't care less?

Can't they see the potential damage to their credibility? Why would people torpedo a relationship that's taken them a lifetime to build? Don't they realize they're undermining their chances for success? The next time these people say something, others may doubt what they say or second-guess their intentions — simply because they're no longer trusted. No one's going to stand up and shout, "You just lost my trust and respect!" but the silence will be deafening.

Some people may say it's not a big deal; everyone does it; no one's watching and no one really cares anyway. Well, I'm here to tell you they're sadly mistaken!

Let's face it, you send a message by what you say and what you do. If words aren't supported with consistent actions, they will ring hollow. Someone once said, "Remember, people will judge you by your actions, not your intentions. You may have a heart of gold — but so does a hard-boiled egg."

Here are some examples of people who live by the philosophy, "Do As I Say, Not As I Do."

ALL TALK, NO ACTION

The emperor is all talk, no action. Like the emperor's new clothes, everything is centered on the show rather than on substance. He talks a good game, but don't expect any action or follow-up from this empty suit.

The politician will say anything to win your vote of confidence; this person is great with words but don't ask for accountability. Once this opportunist gets what she wants, she's nowhere to be found.

The hypocrites are so full of @#%^*?! that even *they* don't believe what they're saying. Forget action on their part. They have a hard enough time keeping their own stories straight.

The drifters have no backbone. They make statements one minute and change their positions the next. If it seems that these people are confused or evasive, it's because they are.

The professor speaks eloquently about theory, but that's where it ends. Action? That thought never crossed her mind. Friedrich Engels had it right when he said, "An ounce of action is worth a ton of theory."

The zombie is so oblivious to reality he doesn't even realize that his words are out of step with his actions. It only takes someone else to shine a bright light on this fellow to expose his insincerity.

ACTIONS MATTER: DO AS I DO, NOT AS I SAY

Whether you're a leader motivating the "troops," a role model influencing your "fans," or a parent showing that you care, it's critical to send straight-forward messages. If your words aren't consistent with your actions, you're not only confusing the listener, you may also be causing irreparable damage to your credibility.

Trust is based on the sum of the words AND actions that you send during the life of a relationship. In the early stages of a relationship, we extend ourselves in small ways and observe responses to our actions. Then we take appropriate action, engaging further or withdrawing a bit each time, until a level of trust is formed. Once we get to know someone, we look for regular and consistent patterns of behavior because the more predictable people are, the more comfort we have with them.

We ask ourselves: "Do they feel strongly about their beliefs one day and abandon them the next?" "Do they expect others to live by one set of rules while they live by another?" "Do they make promises only to break them?"

When you "walk the talk," your behavior becomes a catalyst for people's trust and faith in you. And it also emphasizes what you stand for.

The bottom line is simply this: Trust is not guaranteed, and it can't be won overnight. Trust must be carefully developed, vigorously nurtured, and constantly reinforced. And, although trust may take a long time to develop, it can be lost through a single action — once lost, it can be very difficult to re-establish.

So, any time you make a claim, no matter how small, and display inconsistent behavior, you shatter the comfort zone — and weaken your bond of trust with others. As a result, anything thought to be predictable in the future may be treated as suspect. The fact is, everything you do in life sends a message. So, make sure to practice what you preach. As Ben Franklin said, "Well done is better than well said." **:)**

Everyone on this earth
was born for a reason,
what's yours?

THE BEST GRADUATION SPEECH ... NEVER GIVEN

This graduation speech is for those of you who are going to change the world, as well as for those who are going change the world around you.

This is an exciting time. The world is at your fingertips. The question is: What are you going to make of this opportunity? The answer is: That's totally up to you. Here are nine valuable lessons to serve as guideposts for your journey through life.

9 VALUABLE LESSONS UPON GRADUATION

Pursue your passion. Don't be a spectator in the game of life. Get off the couch and make your mark. Don't lose sleep about what might happen, don't worry about what people might say, and please don't let anything or anyone extinguish your flame. Life isn't a dress rehearsal. You won't be successful if you don't try. So pursue your passion, follow your dreams, and make it happen. The truth is, *some people don't live…they merely exist.*

Keep life in perspective. Many of us take each day as it comes and then seem surprised to find where life has taken us. The fact is, we drive ourselves crazy with the demanding schedules that we keep. It's as though we measure success by the quantity of our daily activities rather than the quality of our lives. So don't get swept away in the current of life. The truth is, *checking items off a to-do list doesn't determine progress; focusing on your priorities is what counts.*

Hit lots of singles. Some people believe the only way to achieve success is to swing for the fence. The fact is, you don't always have to hit the ball out of the park. If you're trying to save money, lose weight, or achieve any worthwhile goal, don't discount the power of taking small steps. The truth is, *success isn't only about doing big things; it's the cumulative effect of doing the right, little things each and every day.*

Give it all you've got. You often have a choice between enriching your life and supporting others. What many folks don't realize is that being a taker is a losing game. The fact is, good spouses aren't self-centered; they put their spouse's needs ahead of their own. Good friends aren't selfish; they'll lend a dime even when it's their last penny. And good business partners aren't greedy; they create win-win relationships rather than trying to gain the upper hand. The truth is, *giving is like a boomerang — it often finds its way back to you.*

Make a difference. Be a positive force in people's lives. It doesn't require a gift from your wallet, but rather a caring heart. Make people feel special; bring out the best in them; and be genuinely happy for their achievements. The truth is, *success isn't measured by what you accumulate in life, but by what you give to others.*

Appreciate what you have. Some people are like sharks that spend their whole life consuming. The problem is, these folks are so focused on attaining more that they lose what's valuable by taking it for granted. So appreciate what you have before it becomes what you had. The truth is, *happy people don't necessarily have more; they're just satisfied with what they do have.*

Own your life. You'll be faced with decisions every day. You have the freedom to choose the direction that you take, to determine the choices that you'll make, and to decide how hard you're willing to work to achieve your goals. If you want your life to be different, don't look to others — change it yourself. The truth is, *your life is determined by the sum of the choices that YOU make.*

Make yourself proud. At the end of the day, it doesn't matter whether you meet the expectations of others; what counts is that you meet your own standards. So set the bar high, live your life with integrity, and make yourself proud — you have to face yourself in the mirror every day. The truth is, *if you don't respect yourself, why should others?*

I'm saving one of the most important lessons for last. **Believe.** The truth is, some of the most important things in life are invisible. Even though you can't see, touch, or smell them, they'll have an overriding impact on you and on those around you. They are intangibles, such as love, trust, integrity, respect, and faith. Even though they're invisible, learn to appreciate and nurture them. They are invaluable.

One day when you're old (yes...over 40), you may pause and ask yourself the question: "How did I do?" Here are clues to the answer: Have you learned that happiness is as important as success? Do you care not only about where life has taken you, but about how you got there? Do you care whether you're living a life of purpose?

At the end of the day, everyone on this earth was born for a reason, what's yours? So find your passion, be courageous, and live with honor. Congratulations on your graduation. Good luck! **:)**

"

We place artificial
demands on ourselves
that undermine our
happiness. These
demands force us to
work harder and harder
to cross a finish line
that keeps moving.

"

THE SECRET TO TRUE HAPPINESS

Imagine…you've catapulted yourself to the top of your organization and reached the pinnacle of success. You own a luxurious house, take lavish vacations, and socialize with the rich and famous — most people would give anything to walk in your shoes. But even though you've achieved success beyond your wildest dreams, have you found happiness?

Some people assume that achieving greater success or accumulating material wealth automatically leads to happiness, but nothing can be further from the truth. Think of the parent who trades family time to impress his or her boss; the high achiever who forfeits his social life to advance his career; the businessperson who sells her soul to close the deal; the family who buys things they don't need (with money they don't have) just to impress their friends.

While buying an expensive house, closing a deal, or securing a promotion can provide satisfaction, these achievements often deliver only *temporary* happiness. In fact, many people pause only briefly after reaching a goal…before setting their eyes on the next prize. The truth is, many people are never really happy unless they are winning, and when the winning stops…well, you guessed it…like an addiction, they need (or should I say, *want*) more.

The truth is, we place artificial demands on ourselves that undermine our happiness. These demands force us to work harder and harder to cross a finish line that keeps moving. Contrast this lifestyle with a life that's rich in purpose and in making a difference in others' lives. The bottom line: Happiness is a byproduct of a life well lived. How does that make you feel?

THE GAP BETWEEN SUCCESS AND HAPPINESS

As I said, striving for material abundance won't create lasting happiness as much as *leading a meaningful* life will. Here's a test to show how your motivations (drivers) impact your decisions, your friendships, your life. Which are you, a success-seeker or a happiness-hunter? You may be surprised.

LIVE HAPPILY EVER AFTER

Drivers	Success-Seeker	Happiness-Hunter
Purpose	Securing wealth, power, and fame	Being rich in character and enjoying good health, meaningful relationships, and peace of mind
Rewards	More is always better	Enjoying the journey and achieving life balance
Satisfaction	Outdoing your neighbor	Being content with what you have and delighting in the happiness of others
Recognition	Gaining approval from others	Maintaining self-respect
Mindset	Taking care of "number one"	Being selfless, reflective, and humble
Priorities	Acting in your own self-interest	Making a difference in others' lives
Goal	Winning at any cost	Doing things the "right way" and having a clear conscience
Relationships	Having many acquaintances or shallow friendships	Enjoying quality relationships
Focus	Obsessed with material possessions	Keeping good karma front and center

Some people spend their entire life searching for happiness. In fact, all the riches in the world won't give that to you. One day you're going to chuckle at all the things that once seemed so important to you — many of them will seem so trivial.

Here's what else you may find. You'll ask yourself, "Am I a good person, rich in character, or am I driven merely by a quest for status?" You'll care not only where life has taken you, but also about how you got there. You'll want to be remembered for what you gave back rather than the wealth you've accumulated. And you'll relish knowing that you found your purpose in life and did your part in making the world a better place.

The bottom line is, you don't have to search the globe for happiness because it already exists within yourself. As Glinda, the Good Witch in *The Wizard of Oz*, said, "You've always had the power, my dear. You just had to learn it for yourself." If most answers seem obvious in retrospect, maybe we're not spending enough time searching for the obvious. Success may be temporary, but happiness is forever. **:)**

A NEW DAY

EACH DAY IS A GIFT FOR YOU TO CAREFULLY UNWRAP. WHAT HAPPENS NEXT IS UP TO YOU. YOU CAN CHERISH EVERY SECOND THAT YOU'RE GIVEN OR LET TIME SLIP BETWEEN YOUR FINGERS. YOU CAN LIVE EVERY DAY WITH GUSTO AND MAKE EVERY MOMENT MATTER OR YOU CAN BE FEARFUL AND WORRY ABOUT WHAT TOMORROW WILL BRING. YOU CAN REACH OUT AND MAKE A DIFFERENCE IN SOMEONE'S LIFE OR FOCUS ON MORE WAYS TO BETTER YOUR OWN. YOU CAN PURSUE NEW WAYS TO GROW AS A PERSON OR WAIT TO SEE IF THE WORLD STOPS CHANGING. YOU CAN REACH FOR THINGS THAT'LL MAKE YOU HAPPY OR YOU CAN BE CONTENT WITH WHAT YOU ALREADY HAVE. YOU CAN DRIFT ALONG FROM DAWN TO DUSK OR LIVE LIFE LIKE THERE'S NO TOMORROW . . . BEFORE YOU KNOW IT, THE SECONDS BECOME MINUTES, THE MINUTES BECOME HOURS, AND THE DAY DISAPPEARS INTO THE NIGHT. YESTERDAY IS A MEMORY — A PLACE YOU CAN VISIT ONLY IN YOUR DREAMS. AND REMEMBER, NO MATTER HOW HARD YOU TRY, YOU CAN NEVER GET YOUR MINUTES BACK. THAT DAY IS GONE FOREVER.

TOMORROW IS A NEW DAY.

FRANK SONNENBERG

RESOURCES

10 TIPS TO CREATE BETTER LIFE BALANCE

Many of us take each day as it comes and then seem surprised to find where life has taken us. We've risen to the top, but regret what we've lost during the journey; we've accumulated fancy possessions, but learned that money can't buy the best riches in life. It's as if we've followed a prepared script rather than consciously choosing the right path for us. Here are 10 tips to create better life balance:

Remain focused and disciplined. Do you feel overwhelmed at times? That may be because you value quantity over quality. Priorities serve as guideposts to keep you on track. Your goal shouldn't be checking items off a to-do list, but rather, doing things that matter.

Invest your time wisely. Resources are finite. When you overcommit your time or spread your resources too thin, you fail to dedicate the attention that your priorities deserve.

Learn to set boundaries. The goal shouldn't always be adding to — it should also sometimes include subtracting from — your daily tasks. While any single request may seem reasonable, added together they'll divert your attention from your priorities. So learn to say "No."

Minimize toxicity. Just as toxic food is bad for your health and well-being, so are negative and unethical people. They'll sap your energy and drain your soul.

Invest in relationships. Studies show that relationships are a key source of happiness. Being a good spouse, parent, or friend doesn't happen by chance. It requires an investment.

Try something new. Don't be so busy that you don't have time for something new. Expand your horizons. You won't know what the world offers unless you give it a try.

Treat yourself. Stop being so rigid by seeing the world as black or white. The fact is, most of life remains somewhere in between. So, if you're living at one end of the extreme, there's nothing wrong with deviating from your habit every once in a while.

Make time for nothing. Being busy doesn't always mean being productive. Set aside time to relax and think. It'll give you time to smell the roses and learn from each experience. It's important to enjoy the journey as well as the destination.

Be open to change. Love what you do and the choices that you make, but not so much that you're unwilling to change. There's a fine line between passion and obsession.

Live life with a purpose. Happiness isn't the result of accumulating things. It's about living life with a purpose. **:)**

11 WAYS TO EARN RESPECT

Authenticity. You are proud of who you are and what you stand for. You're neither intimidated by someone else's opinion nor worried about what people think of you. You don't play games, have a personal "agenda," or pretend to be someone you're not.

Knowledge. You might be very smart, but you don't give the appearance of being a know-it-all. You're curious about the world around you, eager to learn, and hungry to improve yourself.

Integrity. You have high ethical values and are true to your beliefs. You follow the spirit of the law, not because you signed an agreement or are afraid of being caught, but because it's the right thing to do.

Honesty. Your life is an open book because you have nothing to hide. You're passionate about being straightforward, and you're happy to deliver good news without sugarcoating the bad. You don't make promises lightly.

Fairness. You believe in building long-term relationships rather than settling for short-term gains. You strive for win-win relationships, knowing that if a solution isn't evenhanded, no one wins.

Tolerance. You are receptive to ideas, beliefs, and cultures other than your own. In the process, you always try to evaluate all sides of an issue rather than forcing your personal opinion on others.

Humility. You are modest about your achievements, comfortable in your own skin, and quietly proud. You shift your focus from taking to giving, from talking about yourself to listening to others, and from hoarding the credit to distributing the praise.

Selflessness. You give to others because you want to, not because you expect anything in return. You believe that your kindness helps to build trust, strengthen relationships, and enhance everyone's sense of self-worth.

Compassion. You go out of your way to treat others kindly even though you've reached the top of your game. You remember your roots and give credit to everyone who helped you along the way. You bring out the best in people in an effort to make everyone feel special.

Personal responsibility. You take charge of your life rather than feeling that the world owes you something. You set your goals high, make the commitment and sacrifice required to succeed, and accept the consequences of your choices.

Quality associations. You are vigilant about the people with whom you surround yourself, knowing that you win or lose respect based on the company that you keep. **:)**

13 WAYS TO PROVE YOUR HONESTY

1. Think before you speak.

2. Say what you mean and mean what you say.

3. Bend over backward to communicate in an open and honest fashion.

4. Simplify your statements so that everyone clearly understands your message.

5. Tell it like it is rather than sugarcoating it.

6. Present both sides of each issue to engender objectivity.

7. If you have a personal bias or a conflict of interest, make it known.

8. Tell people the rationale behind your decisions so that your intent is understood.

9. If something is misinterpreted, quickly correct the record.

10. Don't shoot the messenger when someone tells you the truth. Thank them for their honesty and treat the information provided as a gift.

11. Willingly accept responsibility by admitting a mistake or an error in judgment — in a timely fashion.

12. Hold people accountable when their words do not match their actions.

13. Never compromise your integrity and reputation by associating yourself with people whose standards of integrity you mistrust. **:)**

17 ACTION STEPS TO TAKE DURING TOUGH TIMES

Be positive. Surround yourself with positive and supportive people.

Remain calm and levelheaded. Count to 10. Try to make decisions based on fact rather than emotion.

Accept support. There are wonderful people who care about you. Don't shut them out, or worse, take your problem out on them.

Learn from the past. Have you faced a similar situation in the past? Apply lessons learned. There's no need to reinvent the wheel.

Seek professional counsel. Identify someone to serve as a sounding board. Gain from their knowledge, experience, and objective viewpoint.

Face reality. Don't run away from the problem; run toward it. Accept reality as it is, not as you want it to be.

Own the problem. Don't waste precious time and energy making excuses or casting blame. Move forward rather than dwelling in the past.

Make tough choices. Don't procrastinate or hold out for the perfect answer; there may not be one. Identify your options and create a plan of action.

Set priorities. Don't treat every option or activity equally. It's smarter to do the important things rather than to complete every item on your list.

Build momentum. Big problems are best solved in small pieces. Tackle short-term items to achieve wins while you address the root cause.

Remain true to your values. This is no time to compromise your integrity. Listen to your conscience.

Be loyal. Don't throw anyone under the bus to save your hide. In fact, putting the needs of others first may supply the positive energy you need to move forward.

Find an outlet for relaxation. Life is a marathon, not a sprint. Identify ways to relax and reduce stress.

Be a leader. These are the times when real leaders show their character. Lead by example.

Never quit. As Richard M. Nixon said, "A man is not finished when he's defeated. He's finished when he quits."

Keep the faith. When nothing seems to work, faith often does.

Learn from the experience. Make sure to learn from the experience. You may have to apply this lesson another day. **:)**

50 SHADES
OF WASTE

DOES THIS SOUND FAMILIAR?

1. Moving papers from one pile to another.
2. Spending an hour to save a dollar.
3. Hearing without listening.
4. Requesting advice with no intention of acting on it.
5. Starting many things without finishing anything.
6. Looking over people's shoulders.
7. Complaining without offering a solution.
8. Creating a temporary fix rather than addressing the root cause.
9. Wading through red tape.
10. Repeating the same mistakes over and over and over.
11. Indecision. (So much for haste makes waste.)
12. Generating great ideas that collect dust on the shelf.
13. Criticizing instead of giving feedback.
14. Attacking the person rather than debating the issue.
15. Creating rules without insisting that they be followed.
16. Worrying about the future or dwelling in the past.
17. Saying "maybe" when you really want to say "no."
18. Requesting reports with no intention of reviewing them.
19. Failing to address small problems before they become BIG ones.
20. Following outdated policies.
21. Making people jump through hoops — to show them who's boss.
22. Starving a winning project because you're funding a losing one.
23. Working at cross-purposes.
24. Talking behind someone's back.
25. Meetings without agendas.
26. Revenge.

27. Envy. (What a waste.)

28. Twenty layers of approvals.

29. Passing the buck.

30. Micromanaging talented people.

31. Casting blame.

32. Looking for misplaced things (every day).

33. Failing to address bad habits.

34. Feeling sorry for yourself.

35. Trying to control the uncontrollable.

36. Infighting.

37. Covering up the truth.

38. Reinventing the wheel.

39. Plotting to gain the upper hand.

40. Dreaming without doing.

41. Gathering facts, then ignoring them.

42. Holding a grudge.

43. Needing to be right (all the time).

44. Demanding obedience rather than securing buy-in.

45. Making excuses.

46. Doing it over rather than doing it right the first time.

47. Keeping busy for the sake of keeping busy.

48. Promoting yourself instead of getting the job done.

49. Striving for perfection rather than excellence.

50. Underestimating the value of trust. **:)**

When you tolerate
mediocrity, you get
more of it.

45 QUESTIONS EVERY LEADER SHOULD ANSWER

One of the best ways to become a better leader is to view your organization in a new light. Here are 45 questions every leader should answer.

1. What three things are holding us back?
2. Is success making us complacent?
3. What policies are outdated?
4. Would I do business with us if I were a customer?
5. What counts that we're not counting?
6. What can we learn from vibrant start-up companies?
7. Are we winning the word-of-mouth battle?
8. Why are great ideas collecting dust on our shelves?
9. Why are we *really* losing great people?
10. Do we read the reports that we request?
11. Do people follow us out of fear or out of respect?
12. What actions, today, will have the greatest impact in 10 years?
13. Do we walk our talk?
14. What barriers should we remove for our people?
15. Do we spend more time building up or tearing down?
16. Are we doing our best?
17. Are our performance rewards consistent with our goals?
18. How are we advancing the values of our organization?
19. Are we *all* focused on our top three priorities?
20. Are we gaining trust, loyalty, and commitment?
21. What's the optimum way to deploy our resources?
22. Are we proud of the way that we conduct business?
23. Are we getting the real scoop or being placated?
24. Do we learn from our mistakes?
25. Are our customers likely to refer us to others?
26. Do we make a positive difference in people's lives?

27. How are we underestimating the competition?

28. Do we spend more time lighting fires or putting them out?

29. Are we all on the same page?

30. Do we bring out the best in our people?

31. Is apathy their fault or our failing?

32. What would we do differently if we started over today?

33. Do we *always* discipline unethical behavior?

34. How can we turn obedience into passion?

35. Do we tolerate mediocre performance?

36. Do we value relationships or take them for granted?

37. What are the three biggest threats to our survival?

38. Do we study problems or tackle them?

39. What should we stop doing?

40. Are we leading or just managing?

41. Do we offer our people more than a paycheck?

42. Are we challenging the status quo?

43. How much time do we spend thinking versus doing?

44. How often do we say, "We should have" when we truly could have?

45. Is there a better way? **:)**

What counts that we're not counting?

28 COMMON DECISION-MAKING MISTAKES TO AVOID

We make a lot of decisions every day. They have a huge impact on our happiness and success. Yet most of us never question whether our decision-making process is flawed. It stands to reason that the only way to avoid the land mines is to know where they're located. Here are 28 mistakes to avoid:

1. **Shoot from the hip.** Failing to consider relevant information.

2. **Yesterday's news.** Basing decisions on outdated information.

3. **Define the problem.** Losing sight of the key objectives.

4. **Learn your lesson.** Failing to apply lessons learned from previous experiences.

5. **To-do versus must-do.** Addressing low-priority activities just to check off items.

6. **Emotions get the better of you.** Making important decisions in a poor frame of mind.

7. **False assumptions.** Failing to consider personal bias or inexperience.

8. **Frame of reference.** Making decisions in a vacuum.

9. **Analysis paralysis.** Expecting *every* piece of information before making a decision.

10. **Garbage in.** Relying on sources with poor credibility.

11. **Fear the worst.** Avoiding a decision out of fear of making a mistake.

12. **Band-aid solutions.** Making a quick fix rather than addressing the root cause.

13. **Ego.** Failing to request or consider input from people in the know.

14. **Take the good with the bad.** Failing to view the downside as well as the upside.

15. **Jump the gun.** Selecting the first option rather than exploring alternatives.

16. **Plunging in.** Rushing to judgment without understanding the ramifications.

17. **Piecemeal.** Optimizing a single component at the expense of the whole.

18. **Fixed focus.** Failing to account for a changing landscape.

19. **It's all in the details.** Giving inadequate thought to implementation.

20. **Silver bullet.** Doing what's easy rather than what's best.

21. **Overly complex.** Making implementation overly complicated.

22. **Out of sight.** Failing to consider opportunity costs.

23. **Deer in headlights.** Postponing decisions until tomorrow.

24. **Cover your behind.** Making decisions merely to justify previous actions.

25. **Neglecting your values.** Selling your soul rather than doing what's right.

26. **Bury your head in the sand.** Avoiding reality.

27. **Forest and trees.** Getting caught up in the details while missing the big picture.

28. **Looking over your shoulder.** Spending more time second-guessing decisions than moving forward. **:)**

Not to decide…
is to decide.

50 WAYS TO LOSE TRUST AND CREDIBILITY

1. Act nice only when you need something.

2. Base decisions on bad or incomplete information.

3. Fake an answer rather than admitting you don't know.

4. Claim to be an expert in everything.

5. Fail to stand behind your product.

6. Tell two people two different stories.

7. Make self-serving recommendations.

8. Fail to follow up promptly.

9. Make careless mistakes or errors.

10. Show lack of care and concern.

11. Overpromise and underdeliver.

12. Bury information in the fine print.

13. Spin the truth.

14. Adopt a messy physical appearance.

15. Offer each customer a different price.

16. Love you before a sale; leave you afterward.

17. Recommend more than needed.

18. Show up late or miss deadlines.

19. Sell what you have — not what's needed.

20. Be inaccessible.

21. Speak in jargon.

22. Make excuses rather than accept responsibility.

23. Fail to fix a problem, promptly.

24. Disparage the competition or bad-mouth your own organization.

25. Compromise your principles and values.

26. Waffle on decisions.

27. Pass the buck.

28. Say one thing, do another.

29. Leave out important details.

30. Exaggerate or cry wolf.

31. Fail to present both sides of an issue.

32. Present boilerplate solutions to unique problems.

33. Expect others to do what you wouldn't do.

34. Show favoritism, strong bias, or prejudice.

35. Bully someone "smaller" than you.

36. Let someone learn about a problem through the grapevine.

37. Accept credit even though it's undeserved.

38. Misunderstand the needs of your audience.

39. Plagiarize.

40. Fail to answer questions clearly.

41. Make rules, but don't follow them.

42. Cast blame at the first sign of a problem.

43. Sweep problems under the rug.

44. Play politics rather than doing what's right.

45. Be inconsistent, unreliable, or unpredictable.

46. Run from tough decisions.

47. Change the terms of an agreed-upon deal.

48. Jump to a conclusion before knowing the facts.

49. Have an ulterior motive.

50. Hand in unfinished work as complete. :)

Honest people
never fear the truth.

52 QUESTIONS TO UNLOCK YOUR POTENTIAL

1. Do you define *success* differently than *happiness*?
2. Do you follow your own advice?
3. Are you excited to get up in the morning?
4. Do you listen to your conscience?
5. Do you make — or *let* — things happen?
6. How high do you set the bar for yourself?
7. Do you spend more time laughing at yourself or at others?
8. Do you make yourself proud?
9. Do you think "everybody does it" is a valid excuse for poor behavior?
10. What percentage of your worries actually comes to pass?
11. What areas of your life are out of balance?
12. Do you bring out the best in people?
13. Do you value possessions more than relationships?
14. Would you be happy if your kids mimicked your behavior?
15. Do you spend more time getting it done or making excuses?
16. Do you deserve other people's respect?
17. Would *you* be friends with *you*?
18. Are you better at giving advice or taking it?
19. Do you keep promises that you make to others — and to yourself?
20. What contributes more to your success — talent or personality?
21. Do you ask more of others than you're willing to do yourself?
22. Do you invest your time or spend it?
23. Are you a fair-weather friend?
24. What's holding you back?
25. How much time do you spend thinking versus doing?
26. Do you compete more with yourself or with others?
27. Do you value quantity or quality when measuring success?
28. How much would you forgo to ensure a better future for your kids?

29. Do you spend more time looking forward or backward?

30. Do you value other people's opinions more than your own?

31. Do you spend more time talking or listening?

32. Is the grass greener on *your* side of the fence?

33. Is learning a priority for you?

34. Do you surround yourself with toxic or honorable people?

35. Do you spend more time living in the present or reliving the past?

36. How much time do you spend doing what you *have to* versus what you *want to*?

37. Do you do your best *some* or *most* of the time?

38. Is your ego bigger than your accomplishments?

39. Do you take things for granted?

40. Do you rely more on others or on yourself?

41. What would you have done differently now that you know?

42. Would you rather be remembered for what you've achieved or for how much you've helped others?

43. Do you put other people's interests ahead of your own?

44. Do you accept responsibility for the choices you make?

45. What would it take for you to compromise your integrity?

46. Are you more talk or more action?

47. Do you enjoy your own company?

48. Do you collect things or moments?

49. Do you actively try to better yourself?

50. Do you learn from your mistakes?

51. Do you give more than you take?

52. Are you a good role model? **:)**

Your life is determined
by the sum of the
choices that YOU make.

50 INSANE MISTAKES COMPANIES MAKE

1. Holding meetings for the sake of holding meetings.
2. Adopting a compensation plan that no one understands.
3. Copying the competition, yet expecting to surpass them.
4. Treating employees as a cost rather than as an asset.
5. Failing to reprimand unethical behavior for fear of short-term consequences.
6. Increasing executive compensation *while* cutting employee salaries.
7. Trying to "fake" the ability to deliver a service.
8. Introducing a new technology without teaching employees how to use it.
9. Valuing a one-time sales transaction over a lasting customer relationship.
10. Promoting a person with good performance but poor integrity.
11. Failing to implement improvements because they're deemed to be too small.
12. Starving key initiatives because resources are spread equally across the board.
13. Preaching from an ivory tower about what the "real world" is like to people in the trenches.
14. Failing to reward an exceptional performer more than a mediocre one.
15. Terminating an employee via email or voicemail.
16. Assuming that communication can be controlled.
17. Failing to offer constructive input during employee evaluations.
18. Encouraging innovation while penalizing failure.
19. Failing to recognize the connection between happy at home, happy at work.
20. Allowing plenty of time to fix problems but not enough time to do it right in the first place.
21. Failing to recognize the cost of mistrust, bureaucracy, and red tape.
22. Taking employees and customers for granted.
23. Believing that money is the *only* motivator.
24. Failing to capitalize on the power of word of mouth.
25. Working hard to attract new customers while doing little to keep them.
26. Believing strongly in maintaining equipment but not in training employees.

27. Talking about the best thing to do but then failing to do it.

28. Spending an exorbitant amount of time and effort on internal presentations.

29. Failing to unleash the entrepreneurial spirit of employees.

30. Maintaining multiple business units that work at cross-purposes with each other.

31. Promoting people based on politics rather than ability and performance.

32. Spending heavily on advertising while cutting customer service.

33. Rewarding "yes" people and then expecting fresh ideas.

34. Making everything a priority, which means that nothing is a priority.

35. Managing by assumption rather than basing decisions on real information.

36. Making promises knowing they can't be fulfilled.

37. Fighting progress by saying, "We've always done it this way."

38. Thinking they can cut their way to greatness.

39. Spending more time putting out fires than lighting them.

40. Adding quality control inspectors rather than designing properly from the start.

41. Trying to control the uncontrollable.

42. Allowing one person to undo what someone else just completed.

43. Failing to communicate the rationale behind decisions.

44. Taking action without first understanding the situation.

45. Failing to monitor corporate vital signs.

46. Beating up suppliers and then expecting their loyalty.

47. Introducing performance rewards that are inconsistent with business goals.

48. Addressing all areas of cost except apathy.

49. Saying "yes" to low-priority opportunities.

50. Enforcing rules that everyone knows don't make sense. :)

Some people
set the bar so low
you can trip over it.

52 WAYS TO BE RICH WITHOUT BEING WEALTHY

1. Remain rich in moral character.
2. Marry the love of your life.
3. Stand up for your beliefs.
4. Achieve life balance.
5. Enjoy quality family time.
6. Cherish freedom.
7. Feel comfortable being yourself.
8. Make a difference in others' lives.
9. Follow your own advice.
10. Build win-win relationships.
11. Strive to become a better person.
12. Make memories.
13. Be a trusted friend.
14. Remain honest with yourself.
15. Enjoy a passion for life.
16. Say "yes" because you want to.
17. Raise good kids.
18. Live with honor.
19. Make others feel special.
20. Have faith in something greater than yourself.
21. Live within your means.
22. Do things for the right reasons.
23. Earn the respect of your peers.
24. Enjoy being guilt-free.
25. Have a small bucket list.
26. Work hard and achieve your goals.
27. Have a sense of purpose.
28. Think the grass is greener on your side of the fence.

29. See the good in others.

30. Feel proud of yourself.

31. Beat the odds.

32. Form your own opinions.

33. Receive a clean bill of health.

34. Have few regrets.

35. Be happy for the success of others.

36. Feel comfortable being alone.

37. Give thanks for the little things.

38. Enjoy worry-free days.

39. Celebrate many anniversaries.

40. Achieve success with humility and grace.

41. Be a positive role model.

42. Live in the present.

43. Believe.

44. Maintain self-respect.

45. Bring out the best in others.

46. Build close friendships.

47. Fulfill your potential.

48. Help those in need.

49. Rarely worry about making ends meet.

50. Remain self-reliant.

51. Give more than you take.

52. Go to bed with a clear conscience. **:)**

"

Moments don't last forever, but their memories do.

"

8 WAYS TO BUILD A GREAT REPUTATION

Protect your reputation like it's the most valuable asset you own. Because it is! Here are eight actions that you can take, right now, to build and defend your reputation:

Do what's right. Values matter. Operate with integrity at all times. Period. That way, you'll never have to look over your shoulder to see who's watching.

Stand for something. Maintain the strength of your ideas and principles.

Be consistent. When your behavior is steady and reliable, your actions become predictable. This enables people to form an impression of you and anticipate future behavior.

Take pride in what you do. If you're not proud of what you're doing, either you're not finished yet, or what you're doing is not worthy of your best self.

Accept responsibility for your actions. If you wouldn't be proud to see your words or actions in a headline, don't say them or do them. If things go wrong despite your best intentions, don't hide out. Face the music with an apology and your plan to do better.

Think before you act. Count to 10 before losing your temper, sending a flaming email, or making a caustic remark — or you may live to regret it.

Be a good-reputation ambassador. Help others build and sustain their reputations by acknowledging their good works, by modeling good behaviors yourself, and by never engaging in reputation assassination.

Let your conscience be your guide. Listen to your conscience. That's why you have one. :)

46 WAYS TO IMPROVE RELATIONSHIPS AND FOSTER TEAMWORK

Are you looking to build bridges between people? Here are 46 ways to improve relationships and foster teamwork.

1. Set the right tone.

2. Promote win-win versus win-lose.

3. Focus as much on the process as on the end result.

4. Expect to date before getting married.

5. Emphasize what *can* be achieved rather than what *can't*.

6. Be the first to give of yourself.

7. Work hard individually; benefit mutually.

8. Assume that others have your best interests at heart.

9. Secure small wins to build momentum.

10. Look at things from others' perspectives.

11. Spend as much time listening as hearing.

12. Ensure that everyone is on the same page.

13. Show as much respect as you want to receive in return.

14. Compliment people in public; criticize them in private.

15. Listen to others' thoughts before presenting yours.

16. Protect everything said in confidence.

17. Build on mutual agreement and areas of common interest.

18. Lead through buy-in rather than intimidation.

19. Spend equal time understanding and persuading.

20. Celebrate as a team.

21. Discourage cliques.

22. Be open, honest, and transparent.

23. Encourage "we" rather than "us versus them."

24. Discourage grandstanding.

25. Never back anyone into a corner.

26. Forge a relationship built on trust.

27. Don't succumb to pettiness.

28. Maintain momentum.

29. Don't make backroom deals.

30. Prohibit destructive behavior.

31. Play nice or don't play.

32. Be fair at all costs.

33. Keep your promises.

34. Make everyone look good.

35. Separate the issue from the person.

36. Never win at the expense of the relationship.

37. Watch others' backs and they'll watch yours in return.

38. Park your ego outside.

39. Find the merit in others' arguments.

40. Take the high ground — especially when you have the upper hand.

41. Compromise your position, but not your principles.

42. Be civil and respectful of others' views.

43. Demonstrate good faith.

44. Prove your intentions through actions rather than words.

45. When in doubt, do what's right.

46. Remember, trust takes a long time to develop, but it can be lost in seconds. :)

Without trust,
no company can ever
hope for excellence.

BELIEVE

SOME THINGS ARE IMPOSSIBLE, UNTIL THEY'RE NOT.
BELIEVE!

CLOSE YOUR EYES AND HAVE A LITTLE FAITH IN A POWER HIGHER THAN YOURSELF. THINGS WORK OUT FOR NO APPARENT REASON.

WHEN YOU LEAST EXPECT IT, THE STARS WILL ALIGN, AND MAGIC WILL FILL THE AIR. YOUR DREAMS WILL BE BORN AT THE INTERSECTION OF HOPE AND REALITY. YOU WON'T FIND AN EXPLANATION FOR WHY, BECAUSE IT MAY DEFY ALL LOGIC AND REASON.

REMEMBER THAT LIFE UNFOLDS IN MYSTERIOUS WAYS. YESTERDAY YOU HOPED FOR A MIRACLE . . . TODAY IT BECAME A REALITY.

WHEN YOUR MIRACLE IS BORN, PINCH YOURSELF TO MAKE SURE THAT IT'S REAL. IT DOESN'T MATTER WHY IT HAPPENED. THE IMPORTANT THING IS THAT IT DID.

IF YOU'RE LOOKING FOR THE IMPOSSIBLE TO COME YOUR WAY, HAVE A LITTLE FAITH. SOME OF US DON'T BELIEVE IN MIRACLES, BUT FOR SOME OF US, THEY OCCUR EVERY DAY. IT MIGHT AS WELL BE YOURS.
BELIEVE!

FRANK SONNENBERG

ABOUT
THE AUTHOR

Frank Sonnenberg is an award-winning author. He has written six books and over 300 articles. Frank was recently named one of "America's Top 100 Thought Leaders" and nominated as one of "America's Most Influential Small Business Experts." Frank has served on several boards and has consulted to some of the largest and most respected companies in the world. Additionally, *FrankSonnenbergOnline.com* was named among the "Best 21st Century Leadership Blogs" and among the "Top 100 Socially-Shared Leadership Blogs."

37773287R00176

Made in the USA
Middletown, DE
05 December 2016